The Final Warning

ISBN 0-9708598-9-9

The Final Warning

Your Survival Guide
To The New Millennium

by
Kathleen Keating

Visit Our Website!
www.countingcouppress.com

Published by Counting Coup Press, Inc.
PO Box 352
Ainsworth, NE 69210

Cover Artwork Designed by Colleen Johnston

This edition published 2001
by Counting Coup Press, Inc.

ISBN 0-9708598-9-9

Printed in the United States of America

For The Immaculate Heart

Table of Contents

Foreword

My first introduction to the end-times came when I was in first grade. I remembered where I was sitting in the classroom when Sister Celine Marie told us that America would some day be invaded by the Chinese and that many Americans would be killed. She even went so far as to say that the heads of the victims would be stuck on lightpoles for everyone to see. That was a terrifying lesson for any six- or seven-year-old.

The topic at the dinner table that night was, of course, what I had learned in school. My father cut his steak, focusing only on the plate. He tried not to show much of a reaction at all. Dad mumbled something about the whole world being on edge because of the Cold War. At the time, my father was an agnostic and felt very uncomfortable with anything the nuns would have to say.

However, my grandmother gave a wink to my mother, a sign that the two of them would talk about my revelation later. They smiled at me and reassured me that everything would be all right. Then the subject was quickly changed.

Several years later, the six-day war broke out and televisions throughout the neighborhood blared the same story. For a week we focused on the war and the United Nations meetings. I felt a sense of foreboding as did my mother and grandmother. Thinking back to that scary week,

I remembered the hushed conversations that transpired while I sat in front of the tube hoping the regularly scheduled cartoons would be aired.

As an adult, I asked my mother about those conversations and the anxiety over a war halfway around the world. She told me that the nuns she had in school told her about the Apocalypse. They too had mentioned the United States being attacked but they also mentioned much more. Apparently, my mother felt the signs for the Second Coming were blossoming all around us. Obviously, this was not something she wanted to discuss, so we didn't linger on the subject. Mother was filled with mixed emotions over the signs. In a way, she was happy about Jesus' return, but was very insecure about the prospect of enduring the tribulation prior to seeing Him. Knowing more details than I about that Second Coming, she quickly summed up her fears about what would happen and told me she hoped she would never see the coming terror. We never really discussed it again, but I will always remember the look in her eyes when she talked about the end-times.

That look returned when Anwar Sadat was assassinated and again when the space shuttle Challenger blew up. It was shortly after that that my mother packed her spiritual bags. In a few months she was gone, blessedly taken before the final countdown.

I put the end-times behind me for a while, lost in everyday struggles. Yet the news and the television shows like Jack Van Impe Presents captured my attention. The correlation between the Bible and the breaking news was so strong that I could no longer deny their relationship to one another or how prophecy and politics were inextricably chained together. This seemingly odd couple had even linked itself to each one of us whether we knew it or not.

Working on a story about an apparent government cover-up, I found sources and evidence that revealed just how chummy prophecy and politics were with one another. I discovered that their peculiar marriage would never end with a trial separation or even divorce but, rather, it would be dissolved only by death, the death of three fourths of the world's population.

I cultivated sources on both sides of the "family" and was eventually convinced that we are headed for some horrendous times. Whether you follow the trail from one side or the other, the two invariably meet in the middle.

My religious sources, various seers who are currently receiving messages from Heaven absolutely corroborate my government sources forming a shocking conclusion.

This book lists those sources, their messages and my intelligence gathering in a simple, easy to understand format. The case is stated, analyzed and verified for the reader in hopes that this survival guide will have use during the dark days ahead.

Although the reader will have to judge for themselves about the veracity of the messages contained in this book, I have chosen to list seers who have a proven track record. Naturally, not all the seers listed here are popular, or necessarily approved. However, they all have credibility, even if the people surrounding them do not.

One such visionary, Veronica Lueken, now deceased, had received more than her share of bad press and maligning from her detractors. This was due largely in part to the announcement by Bishop Mugavero that he didn't feel her messages were valid. The now deceased bishop made claims that a lengthy investigation of Mrs. Lueken and her visions had come up empty. In actuality, there was no investigation of Mrs. Lueken. It never happened.

This goes against the Catholic Church and the investigation process, particularly Section 50 of Canon Law which states: *"Before issuing an individual decree an authority should seek out the necessary information and proofs, and also hear those whose rights can be injured, insofar as this is possible."*

No findings can ever be issued without a full examination of the seer, their physical and emotional state along with the contents of the messages. Any claimed miracles resulting from apparition sites, in this case St. Robert Bellarmine Church in Queens, NY, must be investigated. The reported miracles and there have been many, were not researched or examined. They were dismissed.

Many have shunned Mrs. Lueken's messages, but the messages themselves have been validated when compared with similar messages given to other visionaries. Although in the early seventies these messages seemed perhaps far-fetched, the sincerity of their content has been maintained. The truth was something Bishop Mugavero never wanted to acknowledge. Whether or not the Bishop was involved in the sinister conspiracy against the Church is not for me to say, nor is it the thrust of the book.

Another visionary mentioned in this book is Andrew Wingate. There has been a lot of controversy over his recent messages. However, his messages from 1994 and earlier have been validated by other visionaries. I have only used corroborated messages from this seer.

The book will lay out and debride the facts from all sides. The reader is capable of making personal discernment from the issues and the case presented.

No doubt the case can and will be argued until the final trumpet sounds. This book was written to get the reader through until the horn blows.

Chapter One

Welcome To The End-Times

With a plethora of news channels and online media, the world is bombarded with up-to-the-latest information whenever we want it. Most of us feel fairly in touch with what is going on around the globe. At the very least we *think* that we know all there is to know. That is precisely what a handful of people are hoping.

In a carefully designed plan, broadcasters have agreed to filter, manipulate and disseminate news as they see fit. Truth in broadcasting does not exist anymore, although you will hear arguments to the contrary. Why the deception?

The baby boomers grew up on the CBS News with Walter Cronkite. Was it possible that Uncle Walter may not have been really telling us "that's the way it is?" We learned to count on him and what he had to say. After all, the coverage of the Viet Nam war seemed so up close and personal that it had to be the truth. In essence all that raw coverage over dinner in the 60's and 70's helped to bring the war to an end. The news was real and we all felt on top of the situation. Today, things have changed and not for the better.

With recent broadcasters, news has taken a detour. There has been a concerted effort to dumb-down the world by supplying us with just enough news and never the whole story. By withholding information, coupled with our hectic schedules and shorter attention spans, brought about by the latest electronics, the powers-that-be have us just where they want us.

As an investigative journalist, I would have taken the above statement as a consummate insult, believing strongly in my work, my colleagues and the integrity of the news we report. Our business is one of facts: hard information with credible documentation. You cannot run with a story without total confirmation. Tabloids aside, the news was and should be something upon which we can rely. That is not the case anymore.

Life may not be what we think it is. We are given the "correct" perception of how things are and we must adapt to the lie. In essence, we are being duped into believing whatever is said on the major networks. If a country is involved with internal struggles, too often the media manipulates the real story, stirring up feelings in the general public which will allow their leaders to do what they damn well please. Meanwhile as the bombs are dropped and innocent people are slaughtered, we are force-fed sexual scandals and the like to keep us off the real story, the reality of trumped up wars and fabricated economic woes. The list grows ad nauseam.

Americans seem most caught up in the side stories of presidential infidelities while totally ignoring the stories that demand our attention. Basically, if the story is about sex, it leads and we follow like a pack of Pavlov's dogs. Our behavior is a conditioned response carefully devised to get us to look at world leaders as if they were magicians.

We are looking at their left hands when we should be keeping our eyes on their right hands.

Four years ago, I was doing some research regarding the government on several different subjects. During the investigation, I cultivated the angst and eventually the wrath of the higher-ups in the Pentagon. I had visitors who tried to dissuade me from doing my project. It was the usual behavior from the covert people connected to the black-ops groups and the White House.

You only get that kind of scrutiny and harassment when you get too close to a protected truth. The government never has been too keen on telling the truth and in many cases, the general public really had no need to know.

Notwithstanding, the past twenty years have brought about an unsettling change in policy. It goes beyond the dissemination of misinformation that was so prevalent after the 1947 Roswell UFO incident. Now, there is an unprecedented campaign to outright mislead the population "for their own good."

I disagree with the position of the world's governments and our right to know the truth. The United States was founded on liberty and truth. As Americans we have come to expect it from our leaders. This has not been the case in recent years regarding the disclosure of personal weaknesses and character flaws, but, for the most part, we still feel we are being told the truth when it comes to Kosovo, Iraq, Chechnya and the world situation in general.

Upon further examination, I have found that something has happened to America's sense of outrage, to our moral certitude, and to our intrinsic natures.

As I mentioned, my research has not been appreciated by a select group of people. I have uncovered something so insidious that it is beyond comprehension at first. Yet the story is there in black and white, verified by some extraordinary witnesses who will astound and inform all those who want to know the truth.

With the tremendous success of phone psychics and horoscopes, it is obvious that people want to know the future and in many cases need to know. For some, it is a chance to change their lives or to grab a glimmer of hope that makes their everyday existence easier to tolerate. As children we all learned the fable about the ant and the grasshopper, magnifying the need to prepare. If we know what is coming, we will not be caught unaware.

Should we really know the future? Some think it is better not knowing. The government certainly does not want us to know the future. It would definitely spoil the surprise. In our instant gratification society, many feel it is better to be surprised than disappointed.

I disagree wholeheartedly. The facts show that apparently God does not want us surprised with our future. Biblical prophets always pointed out God's sense of compassion. Due to our flawed human nature, God lets us know when He is about to make a move to realign us. Noah was warned and given time to prepare. Through Noah, the rest of humanity heard of the coming rain and had time for a change of heart. However, the people scoffed at the prophecy. Consequently, it turned out rather badly except for Noah and his family. The Bible is filled with instances from Lot, Daniel, Jeremiah for instance where the future has been revealed by a God who smites for the sake of justice only *after* people are given time for a heartfelt conversion.

Put simply, *"for the Lord God doth nothing without revealing his secret to His servants, the prophets."* (Amos, 3:7)

Further, *"Call to Me and I will answer you and tell you great and unsearchable things you do not know."* (Jer. 33:3)

What do God and His prophets have to do with government conspiracies and our future? Everything. Since the early part of the 20th century, particularly at Fatima in 1917, visionaries and prophets have all had similar messages. We are on a destructive course that will ultimately lead to world annihilation. You do not need to be a biblical scholar or religious person to understand what continues to transpire as we tick down the seconds of this era.

Where is the government in all of this? Unfortunately, right in the middle of it. Since World War II, covert activities have been rampant. So much so that agencies have been created to spy on the spies. Subterfuge abounds and its consequences are dire for humanity and in particular for the United States.

Heaven has used visionary after visionary to get that message across to us. It is not a message that the average person wants to hear. Nevertheless, if we are the proverbial ostriches ignoring the overwhelming evidence, everything that we hold dear - our families, our friends, and our possessions - could all be vaporized. Assuredly, this could all be religious hype, an economic effort to fill the pews and the coffers on the part of organized religion or it just might be the truth, unbelievably attested to by libraries of government documents. The contents of those valuable documents contain our real destination, World War III.

Most of us, if we listen to our gut, can feel something coming, something that is putting us on edge that is beyond any Y2K trepidation we may have felt. There is something else grating on our nerves. Unconsciously, there is something bugging us. Art Bell, the radio phenomenon, calls this feeling the "quickening." I think it is very similar to birth pangs. Upon further investigation, I have found that these pains are getting much closer to one another and we are now an end run away from the delivery room.

Instead of us being proud parents, I think we will be shocked to see the offspring that will grow into an unrestrained monster who will eventually demand our very lives. That notion may seem far too problematic for people but I assure you that we have a very rough future planned.

As an example, consider the warning the Blessed Mother gave to the visionary, Veronica Lueken from Bayside, New York in 1988:

> *Look up and see what lies beyond your*
> *windows; a Ball that is fast hurtling*
> *towards the earth... For even the scientists*
> *have failed to recognize the speed of this*
> *Ball.*

Many people followed Hale-Bopp's journey across our skies in the spring of 1997. Billed as the brightest comet of the 20th Century, amateur astronomers sent telescope sales through the ionosphere. Doomsayers thought they might have misunderstood the Bible and the relevance of the comet's appearance when it failed to strike the earth, while others heaved a collective sigh of relief that we escaped the horrible consequences of a direct hit.

Scientists on the other hand were assuaged that the comet did not bear down on earth. They were fully expecting the 100 million-year hit to occur. Numerous scientific studies done since 1980 have indicated that earth may be ready for another "large event" like the impact that knocked the dinosaurs out of the game or one similar to the Shoemaker-Levy 9 hit that scored a bulls eye on Jupiter.

Was Veronica Lueken wrong or misguided? I don't think so. Hale-Bopp is still very much with us but you won't hear about it or other comets on the evening news, at least not yet. Instead, stargazers have to stay current with the NASA web site and other astronomical sites to find out just what is going on above us. As to what the government is doing to protect its citizens, it has a handful of people who are keeping their eyes glued on the galaxy. The fascinating point here is that there are more people working in one McDonald's than are working on this potential threat. Still, they are aware of the abnormal behavior of several comets but they do not want to go public with their concern until the last minute, if at all. Most sources questioned about this feel we may never get the warning until it is too late.

Father Malachi Martin, who died in July 1999, was a distinguished priest who worked under three popes. He was privileged to a bevy of confidential information coming out of the Vatican and most notably privy to the ever-significant Third Secret of Fatima. According to Father Martin, we should keep our eyes on the skies because he believed a "triple correction" from God was on the way and due anytime. Even the Vatican has its own observatory, actively searching the skies. Are they searching for comets or something else?

Father Martin discussed the strange lights that appeared over Phoenix in March of 1997. He implied that if the lights were not of this earth then our lives were due to change - and quickly.

Father Martin also anticipated that millions of people would be killed during this triple correction. Could he have been referring to the comet hitting the earth? Perhaps, but he also referred to a nuclear strike against either New York or another major city in the United States. There are over 100 suitcase nuclear bombs that are unaccounted for that could easily be smuggled into the United States and detonated. Keeping in mind that Father Martin knew the actual Third Secret of Fatima, it puts us on notice. He was hardly offering speculation about our future nor was he relating the specifics. Signing an oath not to directly divulge the Third Secret and its contents, he could only intimate the specifics.

While Pope John Paul II was in Fulda, West Germany in November of 1980, he was asked to elaborate on the contents of the Third Secret and why it had not yet been released. In his answer that was printed in the paper *Stimmes Des Glaubens*, the Holy Father replied, "It should have been made public in 1960, but because of its troubling content and to dissuade the superpowers from undertaking war, my predecessors in the papal chair have chosen the diplomatic way."

He alluded to the fact that Kennedy and Kruschev were allowed to know part of the Third Secret in hopes that the missile crisis would not escalate in 1962. Thankfully, both leaders backed down.

John Paul II went on to say, "On the other hand, it should be sufficient for all Christians to know this much: if there is a message in which it is said that the oceans will flood entire sections of the earth, that, from one moment to the other, millions of people will perish, there is no longer any point in really wanting to publish this secret message." But some Vatican sources claim the Pope may indeed release the third secret soon.

Another warning or *aviso* was given to four girls in Garabandal, Spain during the 1960's. That *aviso* given to them by the Blessed Mother referred to the Great Warning.

In remarkable events and ecstasies that transpired during the sixties, the Blessed Mother detailed something similar to Malachi Martin's triple correction. The Blessed Mother showed Conchita Gonzalez, Mari Loli, Mari Gonzalez and Jacinta Gonzalez, what the Warning would be like. Although the Warning will be covered in a later chapter, suffice it to say that through the Warning, God will show us exactly how He sees us.

That is an interesting concept. Everything we have done in our lives flashed before our eyes the way God sees it. This prospect lends itself to some serious consternation. According to the girls in Spain along with other visionaries who have been told about the Warning, hearts will fail when they see their position with God.

As if that was not monumental enough, there will be other cataclysmic events that will ensue. Whether these events include comets, earthquakes, floods and pestilence, the invasion of America and Canada by Russia, and so on, it certainly tends to put a new perspective on life. At the very least, things should be rather fascinating if the precursor Warning appears.

Considering the Millennial madness that was so prevalent, why should we believe the visionaries who may be caught up in the frenzy? We do not have to examine merely 20th Century prophets to find information about the Warning and the so-called end-times.

Venerable Anne Catherine Emmerich, an Augustinian nun who lived during the 18th Century, had lengthy visits from heaven and in those visits was told very specifically about our future.

There are also the two visionaries, Melanie Calvat and Maximin Giraud at La Salette, France, who were told of the coming tribulation before the Second Coming of Jesus. In a message given to them, the Blessed Mother said:

> *The demons of the air together with the Antichrist will perform great wonders on earth and in the atmosphere and men will become more and more perverted.*

This concurs with what Father Martin has said.

Another clue that suggests we may be approaching the end-times was given to Brother John of the Cleft Rock in the 14th Century.

At that time, the Pope with his cardinals
will have to flee Rome in tragic circumstances
to a place where they will be unknown. The
Pope will die a cruel death in his exile.

Father Nectou, an 18th Century priest was told,

A great multitude of people will lose their
lives in those calamitous times, but the
wicked will not prevail.

Blessed Anna-Maria Taigi was given this message also in the 18th Century,

God will send two punishments: one will be in
the form of wars, revolutions, and other evils,
it shall originate on earth. The other will be
sent from Heaven. There shall come over the
whole earth an intense darkness lasting three
days and three nights.

Granted not all visionaries are really getting messages from heaven, but the valid visionaries all seem to be on the same page. Even the government is taking notice.

The government, its covert agencies, and some not-so- covert agencies, have a keen interest in what heaven has been revealing, paying strict attention to the timeline given to many of the visionaries for these final days of the era. Since Heaven has never been big on exact dates, none were given, but enough information was relayed that would indicate that the time was ripe. Even if only some of the messages were accurate, it would definitely give one pause.

This book will spell out and present evidence concerning the link among prophets, politics and people, detailing what we can expect from prophecy and the government.

Ties between the government and economic controls will also be analyzed along with the prophecies that detail the coming global financial meltdown.

Subsequent chapters will offer preparations that will help make the coming crises easier. Food and water storage are just not enough to get you through the impending crises. There are other forces at work that will make our lives more than arduous.

Ultimately, whether the future holds danger or not, the definitive answer is survival and how best to accomplish it.

Chapter Two

Politics And Prophecy Collide

During the Reagan administration, the President flew to Berlin and threw down the gauntlet to Gorbachev. In an eloquent speech that will go down as one of President Reagan's finest, he said, "Mr. Gorbachev, tear down this wall!"

The world applauded Regan's words and his initiative, but few realized how much input the Pope and certain visionaries had to do with the breakdown of the Soviet industrial and military complex.

Visionaries behind the scenes sent messages to President Reagan and John Paul II to work out the end to communism. If those purported messages were from heaven, they certainly have changed the scope of intelligence and counter intelligence as we know them. It seems Heaven then has the apex of spies. They do not lie and they know exactly what is going on with the other side. This amounts to an intelligence-agency dream or nightmare come true.

Regardless, the wall came down and the world rode the wave of the pivotal event for years. However, a handful in the intelligence communities failed to join in the enthusiasm. Perhaps they were aware of a disturbing reality. This reality was evidenced not only from sources directly involved with the Soviet regime but also by frightening prophesies which totally contradicted our understanding of the fall of communism.

Veronica Lueken had been reading articles in the daily newspaper about the demise of communism in the Soviet Union and the birth of the new Commonwealth of Independent States when Our Lady allegedly appeared to her.

> *Do not be deceived. Their father is the father*
> *of all liars: Satan. Their master plan is in*
> *motion. Pray for the light. Minds are clouded.*
> *I repeat: it is a ruse. Wake-up, America, or*
> *you will suffer much.*
> (Our Lady December 18, 1991)

Notably adding credence to this prophecy is a former KGB analyst/defector named Anatoly Golitsyn. In his book, *New Lies For Old*, he stated that indeed, the Soviet Union would launch unprecedented economic reforms. Golitsyn added that a new leader would preside over the destruction of the Berlin Wall and a new atmosphere of freedom, an openness or "Glasnost" would begin. Further, Golitsyn warned it would all be a hoax designed to deceive the West and prepare the world for "convergence."

How will the convergence come about? Joseph Story, a Russian intelligence expert, believes Moscow is now orchestrating terrorist activity around the world in hopes the West will acquiesce to the global demands for "convergence," ultimately seeing the necessity for "global structures" to bring about solutions.

A part of the convergence mosaic may be seen on the highly mysterious rocket attack on the US Embassy in Moscow that may have been part of a developing pattern.

Shortly after their attack, two American sports balloonists were killed when their balloon was shot down by a helicopter gunship over Belarus. News items such as these are rarely covered in the west. That may be due in part to the self-imposed news blackout by American journalists. Whatever it is, it is hardly "glasnost."

As early as 1985, Veronica Lueken received messages about such a plan. It comes in the form of a dire warning from Our Lady in September 7, 1985:

> *At this very hour, on this very day, a plan has been built now in Russia to attack the United States and Canada.*

Again in 1986, Our Lady to Veronica Lueken:

> *You cannot believe what they tell you, nor what they print in their tabloids. Russia has but one plan; to capture the whole world.*

One does not have to rely strictly on those messages to see the possibilities. Gorbachev made his plans quite clear. In a speech to the Soviet Politburo in November 1987, he said the following:

> *Gentlemen, comrades, do not be concerned about all you hear about glasnost and perestroika and democracy in the coming years. These are primarily for outward consumption. There will be no significant internal change in the Soviet Union, other than for cosmetic purposes. Our purpose is to disarm the Americans and let them fall asleep. We want to accomplish three things: One, we want the Americans to withdraw conventional forces from Europe. Two, we want*

them to withdraw nuclear forces in Europe.
Three, we want the Americans to stop proceeding
with Strategic Defense Initiative."

Stanislav Lunev, a former colonel in the Soviet Union's intelligence unit, GRU, defected in 1992 and brought with him pertinent information that he later compiled into a book. In his book, *Through The Eyes Of The Enemy*, he states that Russia is gathering intelligence on the President, key members of Congress, military leaders and members of the Cabinet for assassination squads.

The Washington *Post* reported on Lunev, quoting him as saying, "elite troops already training in the United States and in the event of war, would try to assassinate as many American leaders as possible, as well as their families."

Targets for these Spetsnaz soldiers include power stations, telephone switching systems and dams. They are also targeting secret landing sites for Air Force One. According to Lunev the use of tactical nuclear weapons is highly likely.

In confirmation of what might seem to be an outlandish claim, The Blessed Mother spoke to Veronica Lueken in 1987, five years before Lunev's book came out about nuclear strikes.

Russia will go about and annihilate, destroy
many countries. Nations shall disappear from
the face of the earth in the twinkling of
an eye.

Military experts agree that this statement has to mean nuclear strikes. There are some people who disagree that Russia could do this, basing their decision on the purported economic woes of post-communism. The Russian military has not been paid in months. Russians are in dire straights. Many people are hungry and homeless. Crime apparently runs rampant and roughshod over a besieged people. These can be true side effects to a deteriorating economy.

What has happened to the twenty-two billion dollars given to Russia in worldwide economic aid from 1992 to 1997? High-ranking defectors say that rather than paying the military salaries or feeding and housing the homeless, it has gone into the fortification of weapons and weapons systems. One source that follows the theories of Golitsyn and Lunev believes that Russia is making an extra effort to show the stark poverty prevalent throughout the country in order to keep the military development secret. How could a poor nation, albeit a "former" super power have what it takes for world control? War and its accouterments are terribly expensive.

President Reagan had definite opinions about Russia's intent on world eradication and its ability to foot the bill.

In a speech at the University of South Carolina Reagan said, "History teaches that wars begin when governments believe the price of aggression is cheap."

According to the CIA, war is big business and a profitable one.

Dr. Jack Van Impe a noted Christian evangelist and expert on the end-times is a firm believer in the fact that the Cold War is not over. In a 1996 article on Russia, Van Impe writes:

> *As you read this article, 1400 factories all over Russia are manufacturing weaponry for a future war. These arms will be used. Despite official claims that the Red Army has been downsized to 2.3*

*million, intelligence sources tell us the real number
is closer to 5 million.*

*The Russians have one million KGB agents serving
as interior guards. Moscow has reinstated the
military draft. And the resurgent Russian bear
is spending some forty-three percent of its
gross national product on the military – all
the while feigning peace and love.*

Meanwhile, President Clinton has closed military bases throughout the United States and the world, downsizing the military in spite of what intelligence reports state. That is hard to believe in light of this crucial information. Even harder to explain is President Clinton's veto of a 265 billion-dollar defense bill because it included funding of an anti-missile system that would be America's only defense in the event of a nuclear attack.

Van Impe concurs with my sources that have indicated the following points.

First, the Russians now have "Dead Hand" which is a computerized doomsday machine. It can automatically fire nuclear arsenals during a war if the military commanders are dead.

Going against Russian leadership, the military is secretly manufacturing biological weapons of mass destruction. They are also trying to develop the latest in biological weapons such as one project spawning the "super plague."

If this wasn't terrifying enough, the Clinton administration has made a covert concession in its interpretation of the Strategic Arms Reductions Treaty. Under this secret agreement, Russia is allowed to move SS-ICBM's to anywhere in the world. Russia is also allowed to sell these missiles to China, Cuba, North Korea, Libya or

Syria. The only stipulation put on them is that the missiles must be reclassified as "space launchers" and they must have Russian military personnel accompanying the missiles.

At last count, Russia still had approximately thirty thousand nuclear weapons. Unfortunately, evidence suggests that Russia has every intention of using those weapons. Even the Bible mentions that could well be effects of nuclear blasts.

> *Their flesh shall consume away while they*
> *stand upon their feet and their eyes shall*
> *consume away in their holes, and their tongue*
> *shall consume away in their mouth.* (Zech. 14:12)

The Russian renegade Vladamir Zhironovsky boasts of just such a weapon. The new weapon is called the Elipton bomb. It literally dissolves people, but leaves the bones intact.

Since Vladimir Putin took over for Boris Yeltsin, there has been a change in Russia's nuclear policy. To be exact, it is a first strike initiative.

Many visionaries have had glimpses into the future and into Russia's plans. Sister Elena Aiello, the founder of a religious order, nun and stigmatist was shown these visions in the early 1960's:

> *...if people... do not return to God with truly*
> *Christian living, another terrible war will*
> *come from the East to the West. Russia with*
> *her secret armies will battle America: will*
> *overrun Europe. The river Rhine will be*
> *overflowing with corpses and blood.*
>
> *Italy will also be harassed by a great revolution,*

and the Pope will suffer terribly.

Russia will march upon all the nations of Europe, particularly Italy, and will raise her flag over the dome of St. Peter's. Italy will be severely tried by a great revolution, and Rome will be purified in blood for its many sins, especially those of impurity. The flock is about to be dispersed and the Pope will suffer greatly.

Andrew Wingate, also called The Trumpeter, is an American visionary who was given detailed information regarding the probable attack of Canada and the United States. Supposedly, Heaven has given him an invasion map showing specifically the points where the attacks by both Russia and China will occur. This map can be found in the picture section of this book.

On the record, the United States military denies the possibility of any attack of this magnitude. However, off the record, some military personnel and analysts admit that given a calamity in North America, such as a huge earthquake, or comet strike, even perhaps a biological attack, the invasion scenario given to Andrew may be likely. Given our superiority in aircraft and electronics, the United States should not be alarmed, except the details contained in a November 28, 1999 article in the London *Times* state otherwise.

This article exposes a very tenuous position on the part of the United States military.

The Pentagon has ordered an urgent investigation to determine whether its most advanced stealth jet fighters have been rendered obsolete by a simple radar

system being developed by the Chinese,
according to intelligence sources. Fears
that enemies might crack the radar-evading
technology, over which America enjoys a
monopoly, have mounted after an F-117 stealth
fighter was shot down over Serbia this year...

Defense experts say the Chinese, who have
been accused of stealing American military
secrets to develop their nuclear programme,
have used relatively simple, home-made
technology to create a radar system known as
passive coherent location. Yet, if successful,
it could make the worlds' most sophisticated
and expensive aircraft redundant, ending a quest
that has preoccupied Chinese and Russian military
scientists ever since the first stealth fighter
took to the skies in the 1970's..."

In June of 1996, Russia's Pacific Fleet carried out a huge undertaking, a complicated simultaneous test of ballistic missiles from their nuclear submarines in the Barents Sea. Intelligence reports indicate at least fifty of Russia's submarines are now capable of penetrating the West's principal sea-lanes undetected. Russian submarines are now quieter and much more effective than those belonging to the West.

While in ecstasy, Veronica Lueken was taped as she described a vision she saw in June 18, 1990.

Oh, they are submarines, they're coming to
surface...it looks like they're coming off
the Long Island area. Now, as though they've
been alerted to something, they're going down
into the water...Jesus has me watching them,

undersea, and they are going to Cuba. I know
it's Cuba...it appears the Soviets are arming
them."

During an earlier vision on April 14, 1984, Our Lady gave Veronica the following message.

Do not take lightly the reports of ships out
on the sea and submarines. They are there,
My child and My children... It is all part of
the master plan for the takeover of the United
States and Canada.

No matter what vehicle of destruction hits the United States, we are ill equipped to handle the coming melee.

Chapter Three

Strange Bedfellows

Most people understand the inherent nature of the Soviet Union and its lust to conquer the world. Although the supposed demeanor of present-day Russia is docile, the DNA of its communistic tendencies can never be altered. If anything, Russia's foremost goal is to inject their DNA into the rest of the unsuspecting world.

Targets such as Israel, the United States and Canada are easy to comprehend. The resources in the United States and Canada certainly compensate Russian takeover tendencies. As far as Israel is concerned, it is an annoying blemish on Russia's red behind. People in the West acknowledge Russia's foibles as shortcomings. It is a case of the have-nots wanting more.

It may be hard to fathom Rome as a major target second only to the United States on the Russian military hit list.

Rome, however, is the consummate jewel missing from Russia's self-styled crown. Intelligence sources, prophets and military experts believe that the royal jewel is now being cut, polished and measured for its setting in the diabolical diadem.

Without Rome, Gorbachev's convergence and the New World Order could never come to fruition. Rome, and more specifically, the Vatican, will come under communist rule before the final agenda is put into motion. The time is short, not only for John Paul II, but for the entire world.

In 1884, Pope Leo XIII was finishing Mass and was walking away from the tabernacle when he collapsed in a state of ecstasy. The people present at Mass surrounded him. They searched for a pulse, but it could not be found. Everyone thought the Pope had died. Moments later, however, the Holy Father regained consciousness and talked about what he had just experienced.

Pope Leo heard a confrontation between Jesus and Satan. Satan bragged to Jesus that if he had enough time and enough power, he could destroy the Church.

Jesus asked him how much time he needed and how much power. Satan replied he would *"need a century and more influence over those who would ultimately give themselves to him."*

Jesus said, *"So be it."* We are nearing the end of the test period. The scores, obviously, are not in yet. But even if you grade on the curve, it doesn't look good.

Pope Leo was quite shaken having heard all of this exchange. Immediately, he composed the St. Michael exorcism prayer. Believing that the Rosary would be the weapon to defeat Satan, he later wrote thirteen encyclicals on the power of the rosary.

That was not the first occasion that Church officials were informed about such a crisis. In seventeenth century Germany, Venerable Bartholomew Holzhauser said this about the end-times:

> *These are evil times, a century full of*
> *danger and calamities. Heresy is everywhere,*
> *and the followers of heresy are in power*

almost everywhere. God will permit a great
evil against His Church: Heretics and tyrants
will come suddenly and unexpectedly; they
will break into the Church while bishops,
prelates and priests are asleep. They will
enter Italy and lay Rome waste; they will
burn down Churches and destroy everything.

Marie-Julie Jehenny of La Fraudais, France confirmed Pope Leo's vision. Jehenny, a nineteenth century stigmatist had a vision where she saw a dialogue between Jesus and Satan:

Satan said, I will attack the Church. I
will overthrow the Cross; I will decimate
the people. I will deposit a great weakness
of faith in hearts. There will also be a great
denial of religion. For a time, I will be
master of all things, everything will be
under my control, even your temple and all
of your people.

The Blessed Virgin Mary appeared to three children at Fatima, Portugal. Lucy, Francesco and Jacinta saw Our Lady on the thirteenth day of each month from May to October in 1917. Most memorably, the children were given three important secrets, which they could ultimately release. These secrets arguably stand out as the pinnacle of prophetic messages regarding the consummation of the world.

The first secret of Fatima can best be summed up in the words of Our Lady.

You have seen Hell where the souls of sinners
go. To save them, God wishes to establish in

the world the devotion to my Immaculate Heart.
If people do as I shall ask, many souls will be
converted and there will be peace.

Then Our Lady revealed the second secret.

This war [WWI] is going to end, but if
people do not cease offending God not much
time will elapse and during the Pontificate
of Pius XI another and more terrible war will
begin. When you see a night illuminated by
an unknown light, know this is the great sign
from God that the chastisement of the world
for its many transgressions is at hand through
war, famine and persecution of the Church and
of the Holy Father.

To prevent this, I shall come to ask for
the consecration of Russia to my Immaculate
Heart and the Communion of reparation on
the First Saturdays. If my requests are heard,
Russia will be converted and there will be
peace. If not, she will spread her errors
throughout the world, provoking wars and
persecution of the Church. The good will
suffer martyrdom; the Holy Father will
suffer much; different nations will be
annihilated. But in the end, my Immaculate
Heart will triumph. The Holy Father will
consecrate Russia to me, and it will be
consecrated and some time of peace will be
granted to humanity.

At the time this message was given by Our Lady,
World War I was still broiling and Pope Benedict XV

reigned. In 1922, following the death of Benedict XV, a new pope was elected. Ambrogio D'Amiano Achille Ratti took the name of Pope Pius XI.

Another validation of this Fatima message came on January 25, 1938. Sister Lucy [Lucy from Fatima] was looking out her convent window in Tuy, Portugal and saw an ominous red glow that lit up the entire night sky. This peculiar glow was seen across Europe, parts of Africa and Asia.

The scientific community tried to come up with a suitable explanation for the extraordinary aurora borealis. Looking at the dimensions, this anomaly was huge. It covered an area of five-hundred-thousand square kilometers with a vertical extent of four-hundred kilometers. The rays hit an altitude of seven-hundred kilometers and were accompanied by an eerie noise. One witness described it as "similar to the sound of burning grass or brush." Millions of people heard it and saw it; terrified the world was on fire and about to come to an end.

On January 26, 1938, The New York Times ran this:

London, January 25, 1938. The Aurora Borealis, rarely seen in Southern or Western Europe, spread fear in parts of Portugal and lower Austria tonight while thousands of Britons were brought into the streets in wonderment. The ruddy red glow led many to think half the city was ablaze. The Windsor Fire Department was called out thinking that Windsor Castle was afire. The lights were clearly seen in Italy, Spain and even Gibraltar.

The glow bathing snow-clad mountain tops in

Austria and Switzerland was a beautiful sight
but firemen turned out to chase non-existent
fires. Portuguese villagers rushed in fright
from their homes, fearing the end of the world.

Sister Lucy after seeing the "Northern Lights" knew this was the sign foretold by Our Lady on July 13, 1917. In March of 1938, Hitler invaded Austria.

With this validation of the Fatima secrets, millions of people are holding their breath in anxious anticipation of the third secret. Although the actual secret has not been released, just the pseudo secret, portions of Sister Lucy's letters can give us some insight into what she knows. These letters can be found in the book, *The Third Secret Of Fatima Revealed*, by Brother Michael of Holy Trinity.

I see by your letter," she writes to a
priest, "that you are preoccupied
by the disorientation of our time.
It is sad, in fact, that so many persons let
themselves be dominated by the diabolical
wave that is sweeping the world and that
they are blinded to the point of being incapable
of seeing error!

The principle fault is that they have
abandoned prayer, they have in this way
become estranged from God, and without God,
everything is lacking.

The devil is very cunning and looks for our
weak points in order to attack us.

If we are not diligent and careful to
obtain from God strength, we shall fall,

for our age is very wicked and we are weak. Only the strength of God can keep us on our feet.

Let people say the Rosary every day, Our Lady has repeated that in all of Her apparitions, as if to fortify us in these times of diabolical disorientation, in order that we not let ourselves be deceived by false doctrines ...

Unfortunately, in religious matters the people for the most part are ignorant and allow themselves to be led wherever they are taken. Hence, the great responsibility of the one who has the duty of leading them ...

It is a diabolical disorientation that is invading the world, deceiving souls! It is necessary to stand up to 'the devil'.

Our poor Lord, He has saved us with so much love and He is so little understood! So little loved! So badly served! It is painful to see such great confusion, and in so many persons who occupy places of responsibility! ... For us, we must try, as much as it is possible for us, to make reparation through a still more intimate union with the Lord ... It pains me to see what you are saying, but now, that is happening around here also! ...

The fact is that the devil has succeeded in bringing in evil under the appearance

> *of good, and the blind are beginning to*
> *lead others ... This is like the Lord told*
> *us in His Gospel, and souls allow themselves*
> *to be taken in. Gladly I sacrifice myself and*
> *offer God my life for peace in His Church,*
> *for priests and for all consecrated souls,*
> *especially for those who are so deceived*
> *and misguided!*

After reading the above letters, it is easy to understand the anxiety associated with the message. More importantly, since Russia has not been consecrated to the Immaculate Heart of Mary, the apprehension may be well founded. There are many signs that point to the precipice where our toes are grasping the edge or the end of the era.

A pivotal event came when Sister Lucy wrote to Pope John XXIII in 1960 and asked him to release the Third Secret of Fatima. The pope refused, thinking perhaps that Catholics would lose hope and consequently their faith if they knew that Satan would enter the Church and systematically destroy its clergy and the very framework of its existence.

John XXIII died shortly after receiving the letter. Pope Paul VI was elected as his successor. Although Pope Paul never did publicly announce the Third Secret, he made it quite clear what was happening to the Church.

During the celebration of his ninth anniversary, June 29, 1972, Paul VI said, *"Through some fissure, the smoke of Satan entered into the temples of God."*

To those close to the Pope, including Malachi Martin, it came as no surprise. The Pope's words were not used as an elusive metaphor but rather as a statement of fact that Satan was physically in the Vatican. It was known at the time of this ominous announcement that many

Cardinals and Bishops had succumbed to worldly temptations and actively worked with and for the devil.

The Catholic Church forbids membership in secret societies. One such society in particular is the Masons whose goal is the destruction of the Church. The original name for the Masons was The Mysterious Force. This society's first members were all Jewish. Directly following the Force's birth, a temple was built in Jerusalem by the masonry. Upon its completion, they sent their members to Rome and Achea to build other temples.

Members of those two temples were the men who crucified St. Peter and St. Andrew. These members continued the spread of masonry in Russia, France and Germany. However, expanding the membership of the Mysterious Force proved difficult. Candidates for induction were scared away by the name.

In 1716, Joseph Levy and Abraham Abiud changed the name to the Association of Freemasonry. The concept of temples was changed to lodges and that is the structure still present today.

Although the sect has had many changes since its inception, one thing that has not changed is its motto. Found in *The Dissipation Of The Darkness, The Origin Of Masonry*, the motto is quite startling.

> *I, (John Doe, son of John Doe), swear*
> *by God, the Bible and my honor, that,*
> *having become a member of nine founders*
> *of the Association, 'The Mysterious Force',*
> *I bind myself not to betray my brothers, the*
> *members in anything that might harm their*
> *persons, nor to betray anything concerning*
> *the decrees of the Association.*
>
> *I bind myself to follow its principles and*

*to realize what is proposed in the successive
decrees approved by you, the nine founders,
with obedience and precision, with zeal and
fidelity.*

*I bind myself to work for an increase in
the number of its members. I bind myself to
attack whoever follows the teaching of the
Impostor Jesus and to combat his men until
death. I bind myself not to divulge any of
the secrets preserved among us, the nine;
either among outsiders or among the
affiliated members.*

*If I commit perjury and my betrayal is
confirmed in that I have revealed some secret
or some article of the decrees preserved among
and our heirs this commission of eight
companions will have the right to kill me by
whatever means available.*

Although the Masons and their plans will be
discussed in a later chapter, it is obvious that the Masons
and the Church are like fire and oil. So it is indeed
surprising to discover that many cardinals, bishops and
priests are members in this occult organization. It may be
even more revealing to know that several of the cardinals in
line to succeed Pope John Paul II are Masons.

To understand the significance of the Masons in the
Church, it would be important to look at one of the
Masonic and Communist coups in the 1970's.

Pope Paul VI was getting ready to rid the Church of
the Masons and make sweeping reforms that would weed
out troublemakers. He was not entirely pleased with the
outcome of Vatican II, the gathering in the 1960's which

resulted in liberal changes, not only in the make-up of the Church, but its structure, particularly the Mass. Notably, these extensive liberal changes brought about a significant decrease in practicing Catholics, especially in the United States.

Many theologians believe that the sweeping changes may have removed much of the mystery involved with the Church. They felt that the priest lost much of the respect that normally accompanied this position when they presented themselves as friends of their congregation instead of the shepherds of their flock. The relaxation of rules and dress codes, along with cosmetic changes in the churches, were destructive to the faith.

In a document written before Vatican II, the changes and whittling away of the Catholic Faith are very much evident. A few examples of their agenda, which can be found in the book *AA −1025 The Memoirs Of An Anti-Apostle,* by Marie Carre' are listed below:

1.   First, to replace the word Catholic by Universal which means the same thing. But it is very important that this word Catholic should not offend Protestant ears and would not incite the faithful of the Roman Rite to believe themselves to be Super-Christians.

2.   Suppress all the Saints who have not been formally approved and also those who did not have significant success. Suppress also all those who helped to fight against the Reform, because they have nothing to do with our present epoch, in which Unity concerns all hearts.

3.   Later it would be particularly crafty to demand discreetly...the rehabilitation, then

the beatification, and even the canonization
of the greatest heretics, especially those
who have shown a burning, a devouring and
explosive hatred towards the Church of Rome.
It will be better at first to launch a few
"trial balloons" with Luther, for example.
[Author's note: In 1980 to 1983, the years
leading up to the 500th anniversary of Martin
Luther's birth, several quarters of the Church
were noted for their adulation of this man.]

4.   Many are well disposed to believe that
the goodness of God surpasses every offense.
All we have to do is insist on this goodness.
A God whom no one fears quickly becomes
a God about whom no one thinks.

5.   As for the obligatory Mass on Sunday, it
will be well to remark that modern man needs
fresh air and green fields, and that it is
all together desirable that he go out to the
country on Saturday and Sunday. Thus, those
who still care for a weekly Mass could be
authorized to choose Friday instead of Sunday.

6.   Prayer, therefore, the Our Father, will
be momentarily kept. But it will be clever to
oblige Catholics to use familiar language with
God, under the charitable pretext of adopting,
in all countries, for the translation into the
common language, a version in accord with that
of the Protestants.

7.   Afterwards come the Seven Sacraments,
Which are all to be revised, all the more so

because Protestant's only have two.

8.   Of course, the Sacrament of Confirmation...
must be vigorously suppressed. This attitude
will permit denouncing the dogma of the Holy
Trinity as offensive to Jews and Moslems, as
well as to certain new Protestant sects.

9.   As for the Sacrament called Penance, it
would be replaced by a community ceremony,
which will only be an examination of conscience
directed by a well-trained priest, all of which
would be followed by a general absolution, as
in some Protestant Churches.

10. It is of prime necessity completely
to reform the words of the Mass, and it
will be well even to suppress the word
itself and to replace it by The Lord's
Supper or by Eucharist. The renovation of
the Mass must minimize the importance of what
they call "Consecration" and must give
to the Communion a much more trivial appearance.

11. To weaken further the notion of "Real
Presence" of Christ, all decorum will have
to be set aside. No more costly, embroidered
vestments, no more scared music, especially
no more Gregorian chant...

12. Moreover the faithful will have to
break themselves of the habit of kneeling,
and this will be absolutely forbidden when
receiving Communion. Very soon, the host will
be laid in the hand in order that all notion

of the Sacred will be erased.

By removing the mystery, the Masons laid the cornerstone, which renowned theologians knew would be the breakdown of the faith. This breakdown, coupled with Gorbachev's One World Order were deciding tactics that lead to a sinister plot and two murders. The victims were world leaders and the murderers are still free, as we will see in the next chapter.

Chapter Four

Satan Has Entered The Vatican

In September of 1975, Veronica Lueken received two of the most startling messages of all. The first message was received on September 13, 1975:

A coalition of evil is being formed
in the Eternal City, my child. You
will pray for Cardinals Villot and
Benelli – Giovanni Benelli... You must
tell them by letter that their actions
are not hidden to the Eternal Father.
He has looked upon them and found them
wanting... You must pray much for your great
pastor in Rome, the Holy Father, your Vicar,
Pope Paul VI. He suffers much at the hands
of his enemies. He is but a prisoner in
the Eternal City. The forces of evil are
working to remove him...

When this message was received, there was no doubt that it was a serious message but it remained somewhat obscure until the next message was given to

Veronica Lueken two weeks later. The second message briefly details a huge conspiracy.

> *I bring you a sad truth, one that must*
> *be made known to mankind. Our dear,*
> *beloved Vicar, Pope Paul VI, he suffers*
> *much at the hands of those he trusts... He*
> *is not able to do his mission. They have*
> *him laid low... He's ill, he is very ill.*
> *Now there is one ruling in his place, an*
> *Impostor created from the minds of the*
> *agents of Satan. Plastic surgery... the best*
> *of surgeons were used to create the Impostor...*
> *He must be exposed and removed!*
>
> *Behind him, my child, there are three who*
> *have given themselves to Satan. You do not*
> *receive the truth in your country and in*
> *the world. Your vicar is a prisoner.*

Although Veronica Lueken may not have known it at the time, these messages pushed the button on the stopwatch that began the race to the end of time. If the messages were true, the ramifications would be extensive. It is best to look at the evidence to see if indeed an impostor did assume Pope Paul VI's identity.

Four photographs of Pope Paul VI and the impostor are shown in the picture section of the book.

In the profile photographs, the true Pope, Paul VI, is on the left. This shot was taken in 1973. The impostor on the right is shown in a photo in 1977. He has no birthmark. Pope Paul VI has a different shaped nose than the impostor. The nose is longer and straighter than the man pictured at the right. The nose and ear are approximately the same size.

However, the impostor has a shorter, more rounded nose that is definitely smaller than Paul VI's nose. The impostor's nose is curvier and more hooked. Looking at the ears in the photographs, they are not the same. The shapes are different. The pope's ear is rounder, wider but smaller than the impostor's ear.

A better view of the two men can be seen in the head-on shots. Pope Paul VI, again on the left, has a more prominent jaw, whereas the man on the right was somewhat of a receding jaw line. Notice the longer nose of the Pope. Even the set of the ears is different and is more visible.

The man on the right was thought to be an Italian actor. He perfected his role as the Holy Father, apparently while recuperating from plastic surgery. Supposedly, Cardinals Villot, Benelli and Casaroli arranged the surgery.

According to Father Malachi Martin, it was widely known in Rome that an impostor had assumed the papacy. Those close to the real Holy Father were kept at a distance by Villot, Benelli and Casaroli. Occasionally, his friends would catch a glimpse of the hostage pontiff. One friend noticed the Holy Father's arms were bound to his chair, his frame bent. He displayed a sickly appearance.

Other people outside of Rome suspected the conspiracy. A German author by the name of Theodor Kolberg presented further evidence that the Holy Father was an impostor.

In his *Umsturg um Vatikan?* (*An Overthrow in the Vatican?*) Kolberg showed the test results of voice recordings, seen in the voiceprint in the picture section of this book.

Kolberg used the real Pope's message at Easter 1975 shown on top and compared it to the Christmas blessing of 1975. Voice recordings retrieved from the Vatican archives tested the same words in the blessings given to the world.

These two voice recordings were analyzed and tested through a voice-frequency analyzer made by Kay Elemetrics in Pine Brook, New Jersey. The output Type B/65 sonogram voiceprints revealed that they were made by two different men. These voiceprints are so accurate that they could be used as evidence in a criminal trial.

Even if the pictures could somehow be excused as age progression, the findings of the voiceprints cannot be overlooked or disputed. To some Vatican experts, it may have been puzzling at the time that the real Paul VI was not killed. The impostor became well entrenched and the ripples of dissension were fairly minimal.

Some of the duties of the impostor pope were to put out documents and engage in certain appearances, which were tailored to put the pope and the Church in a bad light.

In a message to Veronica Lueken in April 1976, Our Lady allegedly told her:

> *This impostor, who has been given the*
> *image of the Pope, our Vicar Paul VI,*
> *will pose and assume a role of compromise*
> *to the world. It is the plan of the evil*
> *ones about him… to discredit your Vicar by*
> *placing him in print and photographs in a*
> *comprising position to destroy him.*

Injected with drugs that dulled his brain and rendered his body useless, Paul VI endured this torture until he finally died August 6, 1978. During this time, the Masons and the Communists made great in-roads in destroying the Church. Of all the changes made during the reign of the impostor pope, one in particular was of great benefit to Giovanni Benelli. When Pope Paul VI was first taken hostage, Benelli was merely an archbishop, not a cardinal. For his plans to succeed, he would have to be elevated to Cardinal. The impostor pope made Benelli a cardinal in 1977. Now, he could work at gathering support for his election to the papacy. Aligned with the communist and masonic forces already in positions of power within the Vatican, Benelli knew he was well in line to be pope and most certainly, to some, a likely candidate for Antipope.

One source has indicated that Benelli engineered the election of Albino Luciani, who became Pope John Paul I, once it was clear that Benelli would not be elected. It is believed that he did this because he knew the pope would soon be killed. Benelli's contention was that he would not be suspected of murdering the man he helped get elected.

Albino Luciani was a saintly man and naïve to treachery. He affirmed the positions of Villot, Benelli and Casaroli, not knowing that these men were using him. If he did know, he obviously let God decide his fate.

A week after being elected pope, John Paul proclaimed he would continue with the reforms of his predecessors, John XXIII and Paul VI. This news was quite troublesome to the Communist forces in the Vatican. The new pope did something else. He had a physical and he was pronounced in good health.

That physical examination was a crucial point three weeks later when Pope John Paul died of an apparent heart attack. The world was in shock that the beloved Pope John Paul would have such a short reign of only thirty-four days.

His niece, Amalia Luciani said, "In my family, almost no one believes it was a heart attack that killed my uncle. He never had heart trouble or any illness of that kind." (San Juan Star, October 3, 1978)

Some sources close to John Paul said that the night the pope died he was feeling fine. He went to bed early to do some reading. The pope had ordered tea, a bedtime ritual. An aide went in and found the pope dead, his face horribly contorted, displaying his final agony. Beside the body was the empty cup of tea.

Several Italian newspapers published articles raising the question of foul play and called for the Vatican to have an autopsy done. Adding to this air of murder, was the fact that four people died at the Vatican of heart attacks in that four-week period of John Paul's papacy.

Benelli cited the allegation of foul play as "irresponsible." (San Juan *Star*, October 18, 1978). His communist colleagues agreed. Villot, Benelli and Casaroli citing an "Article of the Apostolic Constitution promulgated by Pope Paul VI," denied the autopsy. The decree was passed in 1975, the same year Our Lady said the impostor had taken Paul VI's place.

In October 9, 1978 Time Magazine stated:

> *In an earlier age so untimely a death*
> *might have stirred deep suspicions. If*
> *this were the time of the Borgia's, said*
> *a young teacher in Rome, there'd be talk*
> *that John Paul was poisoned. Nothing*
> *illustrates how far the Church has come*
> *since those devious days so well as the*
> *1975 decree that no autopsy be performed*
> *on the body of a pope.*

Regardless of the mystery surrounding John Paul's death and newspaper articles demanding justice for his murder, the election for the new pope began with Benelli taking a commanding lead in the second ballot, *Newsweek* reported on October 30, 1978. Benelli and the communists fell short of the papacy somewhere between two and fifteen votes shy of the seventy-five needed for election.

Quite unexpectedly, Karol Wojtyla of Poland was elected Pope. Almost immediately, he may have signed his own death warrant by confirming Villot, Benelli and Casaroli and other Vatican department heads. With Benelli maintaining his role so close to the pope, the communists felt assured of ultimate victory.

Many thought the communists were successful when John Paul II was gunned down in St. Peter's square in 1981. Apparently, Heaven was and has been looking out for him. He obviously survived that assassination attempt and narrowly missed several others.

Still, John Paul II knows his destiny is sealed in martyrdom. Several prophets whether they lived hundreds of years ago or in the past century, have all predicted his bloody fate.

Anne Catherine Emmerich had the following vision concerning John Paul II:

> ... As we came nearer, however, the fire
> abated and we saw the blackened building.
> We went through a number of magnificent
> rooms, and we finally reached the Pope. He
> was sitting in the dark and slept in a
> large armchair. He was very ill and weak;
> he could no longer walk.
>
> The ecclesiastics in the inner circle
> looked insincere and lacking in zeal; I
> did not like them. I told the Pope of the
> bishops who are to be appointed soon. I
> told him also that he must not leave Rome.
> If he did so, it would be chaos. He thought
> that the evil was inevitable and he should
> leave in order to save many things beside
> himself. He was very much inclined to leave
> Rome, and he was insistently urged to do so.

Nostradamus also dedicated many quatrains to John Paul II. One of them translates into the following:

Roman Pontiff be on guard while you
approach the city between two rivers.
Your blood shall be spilled nearby, you
and your close circle while the Rose
blooms.

Some believe that this quatrain means that John Paul II will flee Rome and take refuge in France. He shall visit Lyon and will be captured and martyred nearby. At the end, the Blessed Mother shall receive his soul and offer it to her Divine Son.

So what is the significance to the martyrdom of John Paul II? It's been a long awaited event of the masons and communists, so much so they have tried to murder the Pontiff on more than one occasion, as previously mentioned.

Why? It is more than being diametrically opposed in philosophy. Even if you do not buy into the behind the scenes leader of the communists being Satan, you can still understand one of their "earthly" leaders, Gorbachev and his agenda.

It is tantamount to the communist plans for the creation of a one-world religion. At first glance, this might seem to be an oxymoron – communists pushing religion. Gorbachev, however, has that as one of his primary goals.

In a meeting he convened in 1995, Gorbachev got together political and religious leaders who openly discussed the need for a world government or religion and a new morality free from the bonds of Christianity. Gorbachev's spiritual message is pantheistic, repeating over and over that our common destiny is discovering our sacred relationship with nature.

To accomplish his purpose, Gorbachev and his associates will need the help of their colleagues in the Vatican, to achieve a one-world government and one world religion.

First, Christianity has to be eliminated or at the least controlled. By taking over the world's largest organized religion – the Catholic Church - the group would have a firm foundation. By putting a communist on the throne of St. Peter, and linking him to a powerful political figure, they would unite the world and the church into a solid entity.

We will examine the powerful political side of the equation later and look at the major candidates for what prophecy and the Bible call the Antipope.

Twenty years ago, the three major candidates to succeed Pope John Paul II were Villot, Benelli and Casaroli. Villot died in a car accident on March 9, 1979. Casaroli died on June 10, 1998, leaving an aging Benelli. Sources in Rome have asserted that Benelli is past his prime and that the communists as well as traditional cardinals are pushing Carlo Cardinal Martini. Cardinal Martini has been a major power broker within the Vatican and is intent on making the Church more liberal. He and John Paul II do not agree on many subjects, if any. Certainly from the perspective of the world, Martini would appear to be a likely candidate who would relax many of the mores and rules, which have stood for two thousand years.

Another candidate as successor to John Paul II is Cardinal Arinze from Kenya, Africa.

We can look at prophecy once again to determine who the next pope might be and the significance to his selection. Investigating prophetic messages involving the end-times, an interesting message in the 1960's stands out.

This message was given at Garabandal, Spain. When the visions began at Garabandal in June of 1961, Pope John XXIII was pope. Eight months into Vatican II, Pope John died on June 3, 1963. To mark his death, the bells tolled in Garabandal. One of the visionaries, Conchita Gonzales, heard the bells and turned to her mother, Aniceta and said, "The Pope is dead. Now there will be only three more."

Her mother admonished her. Aniceta asked Conchita, "How do you know that? Why do you say such silly things?" Conchita responded, "The Virgin told it to me." She was asked by another person what that meant, would the world come to an end. Conchita said, "I don't know what will happen, only that three popes remain."

St. Malachy, who lived in the twelfth century, is best known for his predictions that listed all the popes from his time until the end. Listing 112 popes by their mottoes, St. Malachy has never been wrong. His accuracy in prophecies make many people wish he were alive today, especially Wall Street investors. Although the investors would have serious cause for alarm if they looked into the saint's messages. They indicate events that could dispatch us into our destiny.

A clue to our future might be found in the mottoes of the last three popes the world will know. St. Malachy's mottoes were written in a combination of latinized Italian and Medieval Latin. The mottoes themselves are cryptic in nature and categorized by themes. For instance, a pontiff's coat of arms, the pope's new name, birthplace, historical events, and so forth. Often, St. Malachy incorporated more than one or two categories.

Dom Arnold Wion, a Dominican researcher first published a list of the mottoes in 1595 in *Lignum Vitae*. Father Alphonsus Ciaccionies interpreted the majority of the mottoes, which Wion used.

Apocalypse aficionados were fully expecting end-time events to begin with the death of Pope Paul VI. Partially, this was due to the Garabandal prophecies but mostly, it was because the new pope, John I and his motto – *De Medietate Lunae*, which means From the Half Moon.

Yves Dupont, in his book, *Catholic Prophecy*, had a fascinating interpretation of the motto and the new pope. Dupont wrote his thoughts on the subject eight years before Paul VI died. Instead of taking the obvious route with the "moon" as did several papacy watchers, Dupont decided to use the Biblical interpretation of the word moon, or a worldly symbol rather than spiritual. Therefore, the pope could be a worldly person not heavily influenced by spiritual concepts, or that perhaps the college of cardinals who elected him were grounded in worldly events.

Dupont gave a sober warning when he wrote about the election of the pope who would fit St. Malachy's motto, De Medietate Lunae. Dupont thought the "moon" pope would be someone elected when the "forces of Satan" take "virtual control of the world via their secret government."

Conversely, Dupont suggests lightly, that the pope may be just an average cleric, perhaps weak and maybe "dominated by worldly ideas, and thus do great havoc to the Church."

Ordained a priest in 1935, at Belluna, Italy (which means good moon), Pope John Paul I was a man always more interested in his parishioners than in acquiring powerful positions in the Church. Dupont had predicted erroneously that the pope under this motto would be Antichristian and leaning towards, if not entrenched in Communism. Nothing could have been further from the truth. Pope John Paul I was very much against Communism and his stance was a contributor to his demise. Pope John Paul I was a saintly man, gentle and loving, light years away from the Anti-Pope he was thought to be.

Instead, this gentle "smiling" pope died as he was going over the list of priests he was going to dismiss. Cardinal Villot confiscated that list. On a side-note, Pope John Paul I died at approximately 4:45 a.m. on September 29, 1978. The moon was waning in its third quarter. Ten minutes after the pope's death was verified, there was a half moon.

In comparing the Garabandal prophecy to St. Malachy's list of popes we shall see if they confirm one another and the fact that history is nearing its end.

The motto assigned to this Pope by St. Malachy is De Labore Solis – From the Sun's Labor. It may have been St. Malachy's thoughts to convey how hard John Paul II worked in his youth. Laboring in a limestone quarry and then in a water purification plant, John Paul II knew the harshness of severe work. Caught in two serious industrial accidents, John Paul II fought his way back to health and entered the seminary.

If you study the Medieval Latin though, the "laboring" sun is one that rises in the east but is darkened by an eclipse. Born in Poland, he is from Eastern Europe. His birth date was May 18, 1920. There was a total eclipse that day.

A total eclipse was again seen on August 11, 1999, casting darkness on the Vatican as well as England, Italy, France, Turkey and Eastern Europe. In Nostradamus' predictions, he mentioned specifically that this particular eclipse, right before the millennium was a dark omen indicating major upheaval for Europe and the rest of the world. Nostradamus viewed this eclipse as a final warning before a great tribulation hits the earth.

Of all the similarities of prophecies, The Warning has the most recurrent theme. This Warning is of particular significance to each one of us. Further, we know the Warning is near because prophecies are coming together, to the consummate point in history. The Pope predicted to be on the throne of St. Peter is in place and we know the Warning will happen before John Paul II dies. With the pope's frail health being taken into consideration, the likely conclusion is that the time is now.

The next chapter will detail what can be expected and our chances of survival. It will also encompass the emergence of the Antichrist and the real Antipope.

Chapter Five

The Warning

If you are at all squeamish or sensitive, I caution you about reading this chapter. It contains specific and terrifying details of what the coming Warning will be like. The chapter also contains reasons for hope, even though you may feel all is lost after having read the details.

In Garabandal, Our Lady revealed to the four visionaries that God would send a Warning. The particulars of the Warning were given to the girls and they were told to spread the news so that everyone could prepare.

Conchita Gonzales has written about the Warning saying:

> *The Warning comes directly from God*
> *and will be visible to the whole world*
> *and from any place where anyone happens*
> *to be. It will be like the revelation of*
> *our sins and it will be seen and felt by*
> *everyone, believer and unbeliever alike*
> *irrespective of whatever religion he may*
> *belong to. It will be seen and felt in all*
> *parts of the world and by every person.*

From what many visionaries have said about the Warning, it is something that in and of itself will cause no physical harm. We will all feel pain and heat depending on the degree of our sinfulness. During the Warning we will see ourselves as God see us, no excuses. God will show us what our punishment or reward would be if we died in that instant. Some people's hearts will stop when they realize their position with God. It has even been reported by several visionaries who have been informed about the Warning that many people will kill themselves after this revelation, but that mass conversions would also take place.

Jacinta Gonzales, one of the four Garabandal seers was told by Our Lady "that the Warning would come when conditions are at their worst." The date of the Warning was not given to the girls, but Mari-Loli knows the year it will occur.

On her deathbed, Jacinta Marto, the child visionary of Fatima said:

> *There is a secret of Heaven and another one*
> *of earth and the latter is terrifying. It*
> *will seem as though it were already the end*
> *of the world. And in this cataclysm everything*
> *will be separated from the sky, which will*
> *turn white as snow.*

In 1976, the Virgin Mary told Veronica Lueken,

> *There will be a tremendous explosion*
> *and the sky shall roll back like a scroll.*
> *This force shall go within the very core*
> *of the human. He will understand his*
> *offenses to his God.*

Our offenses are the main reason that this Warning will take place. It is a consensus of modern visionaries and locutionists that our lifestyles have put a wedge between God and us. Whether it is a society built on sex, drugs, abortion, wars and murder, or that God is rarely more than an afterthought, the fact remains that God is angry with us. As we run faster toward the edge of extinction, pushing the envelope of technology, sci-fi genetics, personal pleasures and extraordinary weaponry, we are about to smash our heads and our over-inflated egos into a spiritual brick wall.

While many Protestants hold fast to the belief that because of Jesus' death on the Cross we are all saved, Catholic visionaries and Catholics as a whole believe that humanity can not continue to offend God six days a week and to render lip service on Sunday without something giving way. Certainly the Catholic visionaries believe in the salvation of the cross, but if you live a life of mortal sin or a life of complacency, your ultimate destination may not be the location you desire.

So therefore the Warning is a gift from God meant to set us straight before it is too late. The Warning is an act of mercy that will precede the coming Chastisement. If the Warning will arrive just when things are at their worst, what has to happen? What do we look for to know that the Warning is upon us?

Similar to Jacinta Marto, Sadie Jaramillo, a California visionary, heard the Virgin Mary describe the time the Warning will occur. Sadie has quoted the Blessed Mother in her book, *The Great Sign*, as saying:

> *A storm of enormous proportion,*
> *death and destruction will strike...*
> *there will follow, as a continuous*

scourge, one disaster after another.
Amid great confusion and turmoil will
the Great Warning come.

Certainly the world has seen an inordinate rise in killer earthquakes within the last ten years, which have further increased exponentially in the past three years. Hurricanes, floods and tornadoes have hit in apocalyptic proportions. According to some visionaries, these super storms and disasters will continue to occur even more often if we don't get down on our knees and ask for God's mercy.

Natural disasters are only a few of the mile markers signaling the Warning. Other areas to watch are Rome, Africa and Western Europe. A revolution will sweep across those countries as well as France and Germany.

Pope John Paul II will flee the Vatican as his enemies will try to kill him. God will protect him as John Paul II goes into hiding. But, his martyrdom will indeed take place closer to the Three Days of Darkness, discussed later. A key point here is that some cardinals will not reveal to the public that the Pope is in exile. Instead, they will claim he is dead and stage a funeral. This will open the door for the election of the Antipope.

Once again, we can look at the list of St. Malachy's mottoes. *De Gloria Olivae* – From the Glory of the Olive, will be for the "pope" who succeeds John Paul II. Why are there two remaining mottoes including this one when the visionaries at Garabandal said there would be no more popes after John Paul II?

It is possible that what was meant by John Paul II being the last pope, as Garabandal suggests, could be one or two things. First, John Paul II will be the last duly elected pope. If he goes into exile and the conclave chooses a new "pope," the election will be invalid. The pope must be truly dead before any valid election takes place. Thus, the world would see the Antipope.

Secondly, what could have been meant was that John Paul II was the last pope before the world would be thrust into the worst tribulation in the history of mankind.

With these points in mind, we can look at the likely candidates for the Antipope and understand his significance in the days ahead and another precursing factor of the Warning.

The attributes of the Antipope would be those that would readily be accepted by a large part of the world. Possessing tremendous people skills, looks and communication ability as well as liberal views would make the Antipope "marketable." That marketability is essential during the Warning and more importantly, after the Warning.

The front-runner, Carlo Maria Cardinal Martini, speaks at least eleven languages, has written some fifty books and is considered suave. Perhaps, St. Malachy did not write the motto for the next pope in an obscure way or using life history to identify the man. It could be the answer is obvious and quite simple – the glory of the olive may simply be the Martini.

In referring to the Antipope, the Blessed Mother has mentioned him as the "black pope." Analysts surmised that this might mean Cardinal Arinze from Africa. However, I disagree. Cardinal Martini is a Jesuit. Centuries ago, Jesuits got a nickname because they were so loyal to the Holy Father. The Jesuits were dubbed the "black popes" not only because their habits were black but more importantly because of their fierce loyalty to the papacy. In Martini however, he is lacking loyalty to John Paul II and this makes him a front-runner.

The Antipope will abolish many Church doctrines and dismantle the Church as the world knows it. By this disruption and destruction of the foundation of the Church, the road is paved for the Antichrist. The Antipope will introduce him to the world. With the introduction of the Antichrist, another criterion is met for the Warning.

The Antichrist will quickly gain popularity and be seen all over the television dial. He will be known as the Great Teacher or World Teacher. The Antichrist will appeal to every religion and the non-religious as well. He will merge all religions into one, as suggested by Gorbachev. Sweeping economic plans will be pushed by the Antichrist, primarily worth-distribution to the third world. So, the wealthier nations such as the United States will be surprised when the bulk of our money will be taken and redistributed to the poorest nations.

It would not be easy for Americans to "give" their money to the less fortunate, especially in the amounts that will be required by the Antichrist. Imagine a stockbroker reduced to the income of a third world menial laborer. Therefore, it might take a catalyst to get us to that point.

There will be absolute chaos in the United States. It has been suggested that either a nuclear blast or mammoth earthquake will render us weak. This definitely puts us in a position to listen to the Antichrist, particularly when he quells the chaos and racial wars that will ensue with the disasters of such magnitude.

Chaos in the world, especially in the United States is an important precursor to the Warning.

Another point on the pre-Warning list, which might elucidate the facts about turmoil in the United States and possibly Canada was mentioned by Veronica Lueken.

She had a very disturbing vision regarding the time right before the Warning.

*I see a huge ball and the sun; it's
a ball of fire. And this is another
ball of fire. And a piece is now broken
off, and it's hitting into the sun. And
there – Oh! Oh! It's an explosion. Oh,
I can't look. Oh! Everything seems so
still and I see people now holding onto
the chairs in their houses. Everything's
rocking.*

Andrew Wingate suggests that we will be hit by a huge comet in the heartland of the United States and a massive earthquake - perhaps as great as 10.0+ on the Richter scale - will follow.

Andrew also believes that the United States and Canada will be invaded by foreign troops six months before the Warning occurs. With such a heavy hit taken by the United States with the comet and earthquake, this would certainly leave us very vulnerable to attack. There is also the possibility of our nuclear arsenal blowing up from the comet's impact, from the earthquake and in the aftershocks.

During a recent interview with Andrew, he mentioned a series of things that heaven supposedly instructed him about, which would signify the coming Warning.

*1. Relaxed relations or normalized
relations with Cuba.*

2. *A major earthquake in the center of
the country, a city will be destroyed
and the earthquake will last much of the
day. There will be constant aftershocks
in this area, causing Church bells to
ring in states near the gulf coast and Florida.*

3. *The earthquake causes oil wells near
the Gulf of Mexico and the Atlantic to rupture.*

4. *The sinking of a major warship in the
North Atlantic.*

5. *A revolution and civil war in Italy.
This will follow the war that has already
started in Turkey, Greece, Yugoslavia,
Slovakia, Austria and all the different
countries along the Baltic and in Georgia.
Lebanon, Israel and Syria will also be
at war. The only country that will not
have war is Romania.*

6. *Italy will be invaded, the president
of France will be assassinated as well
as the leader of Germany.*

7. *After the Holy Father has left Rome
and been declared dead, the United States
and Canada will be invaded. We will be
occupied for six to seven months. The
whole world will be in the midst of war.*

8. *The Great Warning occurs, and all the
wars stop for the time being.*

No one visionary has all the signs regarding prophecy. Heaven has a purpose in this. It keeps the individual visionaries humble and creates a jigsaw puzzle effect. If you put all the pieces of the puzzle together, you get the total picture. Consequently, it encourages the faithful to listen to more than one valid visionary.

Another visionary, who chooses to be secluded from publicity, has an interesting list from Heaven that correlates with today's headlines.

1. The travels of the Pope should be observed.

2. Watch for the financial decline of Japan. This will be the first domino in a devastating collapse.

3. The war in Europe will spread beyond Kosovo and Chechnya.

4. Look for a military buildup in Nicaragua.

5. When Russia enters the Common Market there will be wars arising from this.

6. Following China receiving favored nation status from the United Nations, they will buildup arms.

7. Watch for the comet to approach the earth. It will be followed by the Warning.

Great wars will ensue.

8. Keep an eye on natural disasters and man-made disasters.

What can we expect from the Warning and how do we prepare for it? We are told that one week before the Warning a cross will appear in the sky. Everyone on earth will see it. During that week, we will sense interiorly that something spiritual is about to happen.

Small animals and birds will disappear. Near dawn in North America, the sun will have explosions. If you are outside, go directly indoors and stay there. Lock your doors and windows. You will need to cover your windows (plan to do this when the cross is first visible,) using dark plastic or plywood. This will help keep broken glass from flying into the house during the resultant earthquakes and storms. Visionaries recommended kneeling and praying to God that you will be protected.

Once inside, plan on staying indoors for eight days. After eight days, the cessation of the deafening thunder will be a sign that it is safe to go out.

Near sunrise, the morning of the Warning, a white mist will surround the earth. *Do not* go outside at this time. Visionaries have indicated that you will die because no one will be allowed to view God's power and live.

Voices of demons will be heard outside your house or apartment. They may imitate voices of your loved one, begging you to let them inside. DO NOT open your doors. Be assured that no human being outside would be alive.

Simultaneously, each person on earth will have his or her mini-judgment with God. (Note that the Antichrist will tell us this Warning is from him to get you to believe that he is God.)

A great deal of speculation has arisen about how long this Warning will last. Conchita Gonzales thought it would be relatively short while other seers believe it will last as long as it takes for everyone to recognize that God is in charge, He is the one and only God. Therefore, it is likely to last eight days. Because the overall consensus is that this will take some time, having food and water on hand is necessary. Basically, our personal meeting with God will vary in length depending on our souls, probably a few minutes. These "few" minutes might feel like years depending on the condition of our souls.

However, the comet, the earthquake and the devastation will be over the course of days. Infants, very small children, the very ill and elderly will be in a deep sleep. You should have no concern - even if they stay asleep for the entire week. Do not try to wake them. They will be fine and awaken on their own.

As you can imagine, being confronted by God may cause many people to despair. Many will kill themselves. Some people will die from the natural disasters associated with the Warning.

If we manage to survive the Warning and the slew of catastrophes, we will have to contend with the aftermath of the comet strike. The dust cloud will be so great that the sun will be blocked out and all the earth will be dark as night. Dust from meteor showers will cover the earth, burning the land and the skin if you are outside. Vegetation will die, and those caught outside will die of those burns without protective clothing.

People that absolutely have to go outside need to take extreme precautions against the dust and chemicals released by clouds of meteor debris. Therefore, it is highly recommended to leave the window coverings on the windows.

The dust cloud that will form will be highly flammable and the toxic gases that accompany it will cause many homes to burn.

We will experience, according to prophecy, the mother of all earthquakes, the Big One listed in the Book of the Apocalypse, 6:12:

> *And I saw, when he had opened the*
> *sixth seal, and behold there was a*
> *great earthquake and the sun became*
> *black as sackcloth of hair; and the*
> *whole moon became as blood.*

The entire top upper layer of the earth will shake for twenty minutes. The Blessed Mother has mentioned that it would prudent to pack away any fine china or other treasures that you hold dear.

Sinkholes, fissures, and large cracks in the earth will swallow whole cities. Obviously, phone service, electrical service and other services will go out. Highways will be in ruins. Much of the world will be devastated, but the calamities are just beginning. Something more horrible will occur.

Animals and insects ranging from small flies, ants, lice, rodents and snakes will infiltrate our homes, our food supply and our persons. The animals will come out of the earth during the earthquake and begin a series of plagues, which will make AIDS and Ebola seem like annoying rashes.

It is best to prepare early, before the news media first discusses the comet that will come barreling down upon us. Our lives are due to change dramatically. One fourth of the world's population will die.

As was mentioned earlier, some nuclear missiles could explode in their silos, contaminating the air with nuclear fallout. People will suffer burns and illnesses from the radiation.

A great cold will descend upon the earth with temperatures hitting eighty degrees below zero. The great cold will last seven to fifteen weeks.

As if that wasn't more than enough, evil spirits will now be present, showing themselves to us. They will try and keep us from praying. This time will be very difficult for all of us, but that is the whole idea behind the Warning.

There are several purposes for the Warning itself.

> 1. It will clearly demonstrate that
> there is Heaven *and* Hell.

> 2. To inform those people following the
> Antichrist that he is indeed Satan.

> 3. It is a notice to the Jewish people that
> the World Teacher, or Antichrist is
> NOT their messiah they have searched
> for but rather Jesus Christ is the
> true messiah.

It will be a terribly bleak and dreadful time that will make us all feel that we are at the end of it all, but it will only continue.

Still, Heaven has consoling words for us during this time. Veronica Lueken heard this statement from the Blessed Mother.

*All who remain in the light of grace
will have no fear. They will pass through
this great Warning without suffering.*

It would be advantageous, then, for us all to get right with God now and not wait. Assuredly, if you don't believe these messages now, you will become a believer soon.

The United States has never suffered through a war on our soil since the Civil War. So far, we have been immune to the ravages and devastation seen in Yugoslavia, Chechnya and the Middle East.

It is evident to most people abroad, that the United States is no longer the super power she once was. With Russia and China in the wings, and the Antichrist looming on the dark horizon, Americans need to face the reality of a dismal future and to prepare for any actuality.

Survival tools for the future will consist of holy water, crucifixes, blessed medals, brown scapulars and blessed candles. These seem like unlikely weapons but they will do more good than guns and ammunition.

It has been seriously recommended by many visionaries that crucifixes be placed on all exterior doors of the house. If you believe this is superstition, the following evidence may change your mind.

When the bomb was dropped on Hiroshima it devastated practically everything. Amazingly, though, a home was left standing, all intact. The people inside, a group of Catholic priests, were completely unharmed. No radiation burns were suffered by these men. They had crucifixes on their doors and they were praying at the moment the bomb was dropped. Was it the protection of God or dumb luck?

There have been other cases, one in particular in New York City, where fire ate through two floors of an apartment building. Miraculously, one woman who was saved had been trapped in her apartment by the smoke and flames out in the hall. The fire had coursed its way up to the threshold of her apartment, but it stopped. The door and the door jam were not even singed. A crucifix had been nailed to the door.

These crucifixes and other sacramentals will be of even more value in the times ahead as we shall see in the next chapter.

Chapter Six

Plagues And Remedies

Plagues are hardly things that we wish to discuss. For the most part, serious plagues have not been a part of the North American landscape. AIDS, of course, has been with us but although it has sadly killed thousands, it is not on the scale of the plagues that are scheduled to follow the Warning.

Threats of biological warfare have also become even more possible in this hemisphere. Our response to much of the horrific news about deadly diseases has been to push it into the back of our minds. That behavior helps us avoid getting too paranoid about the "if" this happens. However, the probability of the "if" becoming "when" is greater everyday.

The best remedy for paranoia and fear is preparedness. That is why hospitals have been alerted to be ready for the tremendous need that will arise for antidotes and hospital beds. Most of the large city hospitals have stocked up on the antidote for anthrax along with some other medications necessary to combat the aftermath of biochemical attacks. All of this is somewhat reassuring, unless of course the chemical agent that is dispersed does not have any known antidote.

Recalling what the United States will be like after the Warning can give us a better perspective about how many hospitals will be left standing. Medical help may be too far to reach in the disaster. This factor alone is reason enough to prepare our homes with remedies for the inevitable deadly diseases.

Definitely, there are some illnesses for which the only cure is our faith in God, which, as will be shown, is more than enough. For other plagues, there are actual cures we can keep on hand that can be used in conjunction with faith and prayer.

I will detail many of the expected plagues and give a list of supplies that you will need. Contact information on where to find some of the necessary herbs mentioned can be found at the back of this book. The author is not connected with this company and does not receive any compensation from the items sold.

Some of the remedies mentioned below were given to Marie-Julie Jehenny, a nineteenth century stigmatist. They are included in a French book entitled, *Veuillez-Et-Priez Car L'heure Est Proche* by Michel Servant.

We have seen a steady increase in the intensity and the devastation by the growing number of earthquakes. People are of the opinion that there is little to be done that will protect us from harm when the "Big One" strikes. According to the modern prophets, Heaven disagrees.

EARTHQUAKES
PROTECTION FOR YOUR HOMES

Generously apply holy oil or holy wax to the doors and window frames. A St. Benedict medal should be placed on every window. It does not have to be put in a conspicuous spot. Crucifixes, preferably wooden ones, should be placed on all outside doors. As in the Old Testament, the Angel of Death will pass by the marked homes.

Heaven has this to say:

*When the stronger one comes, it will
happen like this: The houses of the
others will collapse because they have
not been protected with Holy Oil or small
crucifixes places everywhere with faith
and belief. [Author's note: I have been told that
total faith is the key to protection and
cures.]*

*Outside at apparition sites, there will
be no shaking at all. The more sinful a
place is, the more diseased the soul, the
stronger God will bring His mark upon the
place and people.*

CONTAMINATED WATER/AIR

Since nuclear fallout is going to be a very big
problem, purified water will be crucial. You will need
purified water, which has been boiled with the Miraculous
Medal for fourteen minutes. Rainwater can also be purified
this way. Prepare large containers and use for drinking and
for purifying food.

As far as contaminated air is concerned, the St.
Benedict medal and other sacramentals that you wear
(scapulars, rosary, other medals) will protect you. Seers
repeatedly tell us to have childlike trust that God will
protect us.

CHOLERA AND A DESCRIPTION OF
AN UNKNOWN DISEASE

Unfortunately, cholera will be quite prevalent.
Another, as-of-yet unknown disease will spread as well.
Prophecy indicates that medical science will not be able to
combat it. This horrible illness will first attack the heart,
then the spirit and tongue. Heat will accompany the body
parts afflicted and the body will turn fiery red. Those
stricken will feel as if they are burning to death.

Heaven has told seers that there is *only* one remedy,
which can save you. The leaves of the hawthorn can be
used. Do not use the wood of the hawthorn, only the leaves.

Boil a pot of water, remove it from heat and, steep
the leaves. Cover for fourteen minutes and allow the steam
to remain in the pot. At the first sign of the disease, use
three times daily.

This disease will produce continual vomiting and
nausea. If the remedy is taken too late, the part of the body

afflicted will become black and in the black there will be seen a pale, yellow streak.

EPIDEMICS AND EPIZOOTIC (ANIMALS)

Again, the St. Benedict medal on your pets will alleviate this equine influenza that will affect horses, cattle, sheep, buffalo and hoofed animals. It would also be beneficial if owners of such animals were to keep the vaccinations current against such diseases. (Author's note: Equine Encephalitis can be transferred to humans quite easily. Although this particular direction from Heaven does not mention this disease, it is another plague to keep in mind. Owners of horses should check with their veterinarians about vaccinations for their animals.)

Regarding herds of animals, where it many be impossible to place a medal on every one, a respectful procession with the statue of St. Benedict without fear or dread may arrest the calamity.

DURING THE PERIOD OF THE GREAT CALAMITIES/CHASTISEMENTS

Recite the following prayer five to seven times per day and meditate for one to two minutes.

I hail you, I adore you, I embrace you...oh adorable Cross of my Savior. Protect us, keep us, save us. Jesus loved you so much, by His example I love you. By your holy cross, calm our fears

*that we may only experience peace and
trust.*

WARS AND REVOLUTIONS

Jesus gave the following quote to Marie-Julie Jehenny:

*To dispel fear and terror, touch your
forehead with a holy picture or medal
of Mary Immaculate. Your spirit will
remain calm. Your heart will not fear
the approach of the terror of men. Your
spirit will not experience the effects
of My Great Justice.*

THE THREE DAYS OF DARKNESS
(discussed in a later chapter)

Only blessed wax candles, preferably beeswax, will give light. One such candle will do for each household during the three days of darkness. However, candles will not burn in homes of the impious or blasphemers.

FATAL PLAGUES

This remedy relies *solely* on your trust in God that He will help you. Write the following words on a thin sheet of paper: "O, Jesus, Conqueror of Death, Save us. O Crux Ave." (Hail, O Cross.) You then swallow the piece of paper.

UNKNOWN DISEASES

Use a medal of the Sacred Heart and the Miraculous Medal, steep in a glass of water. You then drink this water, which is twice blessed, twice purified. One drop in your food will drive away the disease.

GREAT STORMS

Recite the following prayer: "O Jesus, conqueror of death, save us."

DIVERSE ILLNESSES

For unknown fevers, steep and brew violet. For severe headaches and chest pains, especially in critical cases, steep and brew St. John's Wort.

EARTHLY AND CELESTIAL FIRE

In a message given to Marie-Julie Jehenny, Our Lord says:

*The heat will be terrible...make the
sign of the cross with Holy water to
diminish the heat and drive away the
sparks. You will kiss five times,
small indulgenced crosses...small crosses
applied to the five wounds of Christ
crucified on a holy image.*

For such protection may benefit souls,

*poor sinners, invoking My Immaculate
Mother, Mother of Salvation, Refuge
and Reconciliation of Sinners.*

PROTECTION FROM NUCLEAR
CONTAMINATION
AND THE GREAT FREEZE

In chapter five it was mentioned after the comet that the great freeze will occur and last seven to fifteen weeks. The cold will be so severe that it will split rocks. Obviously, there will be no gas, electricity or water. Use kerosene heaters or wood burning stoves.

Of major concern is nuclear contamination in our food and water supply. You should have on hand one or all of the following:

- St. Joseph's Spring Holy Water
- The Three Kings Holy Water
- St. Charbel Oil and/or
- The Weeping Crucifix Oil of Geno Marti

Add three drops in food while cooking or in your drinking water or beverage to neutralize the contamination. You can also wash fruit and vegetables with a damp cloth soaked with the Holy Water to avoid nuclear contamination.

If you add three drops of St. Joseph's Spring Holy Water in bulk water and other liquids, they will not freeze.

SURVIVAL PREPARATION

Water is absolutely vital to survival. Each person needs one gallon of water per day. Obviously, baths, showers and laundry will have to wait. Hygiene must also figure into the equation.

It is best to keep a metal coffeepot on hand to boil water. Large plastic garbage cans, washed and bleached will store water for up to six months. After six months it is best to empty the containers and start over. If you run out of stored water, you will have to use an alternate source.

In times of disaster, always assume any water not stored is contaminated. Even if water from a stream appears crystal clear, it can still be polluted. If you find brackish water, it is important to strain the debris through cheesecloth, paper towels or coffee filters. Then the water should be treated using one of the following methods.

BOILING

Bring water to a rolling boil and keep water boiling for at least ten minutes. For every thousand feet above sea level, add one minute to the boiling time. Keep the pot covered to shorten the time to reach a boil.

DISTILLED WATER

Distilled water can be purchased in the store, but take it out of original jugs because the containers degrade after six months.

DRY CHLORINE
(also called Calcium Hypochlorite)

The advantage of this method is extra shelf life if containers are kept in a cool, dry place. It may be stored for up to ten years with minimal degradation.

HYDROGEN PEROXIDE

Peroxide degrades more rapidly than chlorine but it is safe to use as a water disinfectant. This method, though, needs to have residual measurements taken to ensure disinfection is complete.

IODINE

Use twelve drops per gallon of water unless instructions indicate otherwise. Mix well and allow the water to stand thirty minutes before using.

LIQUID CHLORINE BLEACH

Bleach best suited for water treatment must contain 5.25% sodium hypochlorite and should not have any soap or phosphates.

For disinfecting one gallon of water, add 1/8 teaspoon of bleach, or eight drops if the water is clear. Should the water be cloudy, add ¼ teaspoon of bleach, or sixteen drops.

If you disinfect five gallons of clear water, ½ teaspoon or 40 drops of bleach should be added. Five gallons of cloudy water should have one full teaspoon or eighty drops of bleach added for best results.

Use ¼ cup of chlorine if you have fifty-five gallon drums of water. This measurement is appropriate for city water. However, if you use creek, river or pond water, more chlorine will be necessary. Test kits are highly recommended.

PURIFICATION TABLETS

This is an easier method that is either chlorine or iodine based. One or two tablets will purify one quart or one liter of water. Follow package instructions.

RED WINE TREATED WATER

Centuries ago, this method was used to treat water. Sufficient purification will be achieved if you add one part wine to three parts water.

STABILIZED OXYGEN

This particular disinfection treatment is a favorite because stabilized oxygen has no taste and has no risks associated with its use. In fact, some experts think this treatment may have health advantages.

If long-term storage is involved, it is best to treat one gallon of previously chlorinated water with ten drops of stabilized oxygen. Should the water not be chlorinated, twenty drops added to the supply is best.

WATERBED OR SWIMMING POOL WATER

Water from waterbeds and pools can be used for flushing toilets but can also be treated as above for drinking. Chlorine testers work well here.

END TIME FOOD LIST

To survive the tribulation, we will need approximately three-and-a-half years of food for each family member. If you have pets, food should be bought in bulk for them.

The following list is based on the needs of four persons for seven weeks.

MEAT AND FISH PRODUCTS

- 4 cans (12 oz) Corned-Beef products
- 7 cans (15 oz) Canned Roast Beef Hash
- 5 cans (15 oz) Corned Beef Hash
- 10 cans (7 oz) Smoked Vienna Sausage
- 4 cans (7-3/4 oz) Pink Salmon Fish
- 12 cans (3-3/4 oz) Fish Steaks (Herring)

VEGETABLES

- 7 cans (12 oz) Vegetable Juice
- 4 cans (10-1/2 oz) mixed Vegetables (or Veg. Soup)
- 2 cans (10-1/2 oz) Spanish-Style Vegetables (Gazpacho)
- 4 cans (8-1/2 oz) Asparagus
- 2 cans (7-3/4 oz) Spinach
- 2 cans (8-1/2 oz) Carrots
- 4 cans (16 oz) Zucchini Squash

FRUITS

- 10 cans (16 oz) Fruit Cocktail mixed fruit
- 6 cans (16 oz) Mandarin Orange Segments
- 1 box (15 oz) Seedless Raisins
- 1 jar (3 lbs) Grape jelly
- 1 jar (2 lbs) Strawberry jam
- 2 jars (8 oz) Peanut Butter (or 2 lbs)
- 4 cans (3 oz) Dried Prunes (or box)

MILK PRODUCTS

- 2 boxes (ten 1/2 qt envelopes /box) Powdered Milk (obtain a 1 qt. jar for mixing milk)
- 2 boxes (ten 12.3 oz envelopes) per box,
- Instant Breakfast Drinks
- 8 jars (5 oz) Pasteurized Processed Cheese-Spread

SOUPS

- 3 cans (11-1/4 oz) Split-Pea with Ham & Bacon
- 4 cans (8-1/2 oz) Peas & Carrots (Vegetable)

NUTS

- 2 bags (2 lbs) Assorted Nuts in Shell
- 1 bag (1 Lb) Almonds in Shell

SUGAR PRODUCTS

- 2 jars (quart size) Honey (and Honeycomb)

STRAINED FOOD PRODUCTS

- 7 jars Assorted Baby Food
- Applesauce is excellent for all people.
- Instant rice, etc.

OPTIONAL FOOD

- 1 jar (20-1/2 oz) Stone-ground Fresh Horse Radish
- 14 boxes (LARGE) Salted Crackers
- 2 cans (4-5/8 oz) Cheese Spread (Push-Button)

HERB AND SACRAMENTAL LIST

(To find these items as well as other necessary spiritual tools, please see page 254.)

- Blessed Candles
- Blessed Grapes
- Blessed Rosaries
- Blood of Christ Seals
- Brown Scapular
- Consecrate the House Prayer Cards
- Ginger Root - for lungs and heart
- Hawthorn Leaves - for infants, plague and diverse illnesses
- Holy Face Medal
- La Salette Crucifix - will glow in the three days of darkness
- Minced garlic - for heart and lungs
- Miraculous Medal
- Our Lady of Protection Medal

- St. Benedict Crucifix
- St. Benedict Medal
- St. John's Wort - plague and diverse illnesses
- St. Michael's Incense
- Violet - plagues and diverse illnesses
- Yarrow Root - plague

Last but not least, a list of important household items to have on hand.

- Aluminum Foil
- Bandages
- Batteries
- Bible
- Bug Spray
- Cleansers
- Contact Lens Cleaner
- Deodorant
- Feminine Hygiene Products
- Fire Wood
- Flashlights
- Gatorade, Juice
- Listerine
- Matches
- Oil Lamps and Candles
- Radio - Wind-up radio if possible
- Salt
- Shampoo
- Soap
- Toilet Paper

- Toothpaste
- Vodka or alcohol for disinfecting

Chapter Seven

The Antichrist

To fully understand the nature of the Antichrist, or 666 as he is often referred to, we can explore prophecy and a bit of history.

Everyone either jokes or speculates about the name of the Antichrist, but how do we really know who he is? The world is full of candidates, or so we think.

The Book of Revelation, Chapter Thirteen, describes how we go about this discernment.

> *This calls for wisdom. Let him who has*
> *Understanding reckon the number of the*
> *Beast: It represents a human name. And the*
> *Number in question is 666.*

One needs intelligence and spiritual light to decipher who the man might be.

Many rabbis have been using the gematria code to aid them in their search. Each letter in the code is assigned a number. In the past few years there have been websites where you could plug in the name of your candidate for Antichrist and the gematria code comes up, be it 666 or some other number. Names that have been discussed have been Bill Gates, Bill Clinton, and even Hillary Clinton. One group of rabbis who have claimed that using gematria, the name of Prince Charles fits the 666. This is an interesting bunch of candidates, but do they really fit the meaning behind 666?

First, let us look at how the number was devised. According to Father Gobbi, the Blessed Mother explained the origin of 666.

> *Calculate now its number, 666, to understand how it indicates the name of a man. The number 333 indicates the divinity. Lucifer rebels against God through pride, because he wants to put himself above God.*

> *333 is the number which indicates the mystery of God. He who wants to put himself above God, bears the sign 666, and consequently, indicates the name of Lucifer, Satan, that is to say, of him who sets himself against Christ, of Antichrist.*

A very interesting point is brought up in the following message:

> *666 indicated once...expresses the year 666. In this period of history, the Antichrist manifested through the phenomenon of Islam, which directly denies the mystery of the Blessed Trinity, [333] and the divinity of our Lord, Jesus Christ.*

This time in history saw unprecedented destruction of Christian communities. The Islamic Military force invaded Europe and nearly wiped out Christianity entirely. Father Gobbi was told that the Blessed Mother intervened and that God stopped the total eradication of the faith.

In the year 1332, (666 x 2) there was a "radical attack on the faith in the word (Parola) of God." The Blessed Mother went on to tell Father Gobbi, "Through philosophers who began to give exclusive value to science and then to reason, there is a gradual tendency to constitute human intelligence as the sole criteria of truth."

This period of time saw the Protestant Reformation. Each new church altered the Bible and the interpretation left to individuals.

Multiply 666 by three and you get 1998. At this point, the machinery was in place and the world was ready for the beast, the idol or the Antichrist.

The Blessed Mother told Father Gobbi:

> *...the door will be open for the appearance of the man or the very person of the Antichrist.*

The speculation about who the Antichrist is will soon be over. All the wonder about whether he is some myth from organized religion and fringe cults will subside. The Antichrist's Day of Declaration approaches, perhaps much sooner than we anticipated.

In fact, one major network in the United States is all prepared and has made arrangements with the Antichrist and his people to air an all-important interview. This interview will lay the foundation for him to become, at first, indispensable in solving our problems and later, to become master of the world.

He has already made many appearances all over the globe, often dressed in long white robes, at times wearing a turban. It could be said he is doing his best impersonation of the Messiah, of Jesus. In some of his gatherings, he even heals the sick. Literally appearing out of the blue, and leaving by disappearing into thin air, he has won many believers. Some are convinced that he is divine.

At other sightings, the Antichrist materializes as a handsome, sophisticated European in his early thirties. Dressed in two thousand-dollar suits, his presence is quite attractive. In this particular persona, he has been seen with "military" males dressed in fatigues. It has been clear to observers that he is the one in charge.

Already he has a well-oiled machine in place, a savvy organization very much into disseminating information about him, not so much in Madison Avenue style, but rather as an approachable type of "guy," who just happens to claim he is Christ, Buddha, or the Great World Teacher.

He espouses the elimination of poverty and the implementation of decent medical care, which are all positive things. Eventually he will push a one-world religion. Depending on where he turns up, whether it is Christian services, or Buddhist, he works at appealing to everyone, to every faith. To say the least, he is adaptable.

His workers are fervent, tireless believers who think he is here to redeem the world. The Antichrist has his prediction list forecasting global economic woes, famine, drought, the works. He also professes that he will not take control until we as a whole demand that he does.

In an interview with one of his staff, I was told that this man would be our only hope for survival. He alone can quell the wars and solve our problems before we destroy one another. Peace and love are his mottoes. A surprising revelation about this man is that he insists he is not here to be worshipped. Rather he simply wants to be a friend, a brother.

Upon further investigation and more interviews, I have discovered that he is in regular communication with world leaders and, in some cases, daily communication. In fact, it was told to me that policies developed by certain governments have come from the World Teacher.

The Antichrist was present at Rabin's funeral, known by the heads of state, but still unrecognizable to the majority of the world. Each week he further entrenches himself in worldly affairs, whether he is involved in peace talks or food relief; he seems ever present, definitely ever ready. Ultimately, everyone will know him. He has websites up and running, pushing his agenda and gathering disciples.

There is not much debate in the visionary circles as to the identity of the Antichrist. From interviews with seers and research into messages worldwide, there is a definite unanimity. But, some visionaries seem to have been shown what appears to be a different person at least in physical description.

For instance, Christina Gallagher, an Irish seer and stigmatist describes him as: "A man in his fifties and looks like a bishop," and exudes a "feeling of horror."

> *His face has a sallow complexion. His hair*
> *was cut short and it was very black. He had*
> *a roundish bold-looking face with very dark*
> *eyes. He has broad shouldered. His looks were*

piercing and penetrating. They were unusual.
He did not smile."

Other visionaries disagree with this physical description, claiming the Antichrist has long, dark hair, sometimes tied back but that he can also appear blonde and blue eyed. Most accounts of him describe him as younger man in his mid-thirties who is tall and thin.

Before Jesus returns, there will indeed be many Antichrists before *the* Antichrist takes over. We have already seen thousands of claims from solitary individuals to cult leaders declaring they are Jesus.

The Bible clearly says that one of the many signs that point to the Second Coming is the amount of false messiahs who will spring up. However, one particular man has been mentioned to seers over and over again. Even though the majority of seers never speak to each other or read each other's messages, they all were given the same name of the Antichrist. Therefore, the information on the Antichrist in this book will be based on this particular person. Independent inquiry has determined that this man is the best prospect.

The Antichrist will be officially introduced as our "savior" by the Antipope who, as a religious figure, will encourage our worship of him. This will come at a time when most of Church doctrine will be rewritten and a bulk of the Bible. These indications highlight the fact that the Antichrist and Antipope should not be followed.

As an example, the Antichrist has taken scripture and has changed the words to direct people to view him as the messiah instead of Jesus. The Antichrist has boldly taken the name of Jesus out of the text. For instance, he has substituted Jesus' name for Esa. Here is one of the quotes that he has rewritten from St. Matthew 24:4-5:

*And in answer, Esa said to them, 'Take
care that no one leads you astray. For
many will come in my name, saying, 'I am
the Christ,' and they will lead many
astray.*

This is the correct quotation from St. Matthew:

*And Jesus said to them: Take heed that
no one seduce you. For many will come
in my name saying, I am Christ. And
they will seduce many.*

A disciple of the Antichrist quotes St. Mark 13:37
as saying, "Thus Esa warned all future humanity through
his followers: And what I say unto you, I say unto all,
Watch!"

The correct version of the Gospel should read:

*And what I say unto you, I say to
all: Watch.*

The sentence above, "Thus Esa..." is totally
contrived.

So who the heck is this Esa guy? To understand
why the Antichrist changed Jesus' name to Esa, we can
look at some arguments by Jacques Maritain, a Catholic
philosopher. His book *An Introduction To Philosophy*, first
published in 1930 and republished by Christian Classics,
mentions fascinating premises that give insight into Esa.

*That which exists **a se** or from itself,*
possessing in itself the entire explanation
of its existence is uncaused; God alone is
*from himself, **a se**. Created substances of*
the contrary (created subjects of action)
*are caused, they exist **per se**, in virtue of*
*their essence; they do not exist **a se**. In*
their own nature they possess everything
necessary to receive existence, but do not
possess an existence not received from without.

They are sufficient by themselves to exist,
in the strictly qualified sense that they do
not exist as something which belongs to
something else, but, absolutely speaking, they
are by no means a sufficient ground of their own
existence.

This is a very complicated passage. Now the next quote from Maritain makes the case for what the Antichrist is trying to do in a much easier explanation.

*That which is **a se** cannot cease*
*to exist; that which **per se** without*
*being **a se** can lose its existence.*

Therefore, mere man exists *in se* and *per se* but not *a se*. Only God exists *a se*. The reverse of God or the uncreated (*a se*) is the created Esa, or *a se* reversed. This name is a vain attempt to show that Esa – or the correct name Jesus – is merely created and not God. That is blasphemy in Christian doctrine.

By referring to Jesus as merely a man, the Antichrist denies Jesus is God and God's only begotten son. Does a man who removes Jesus' name from sacred scripture, denying He is God's son automatically become a candidate for Antichrist?

The Bible makes this act quite clear in I John 2: 22-23:

Who is a liar, but he who denieth
that Jesus is the Christ? This is the
Antichrist, who denieth the Father
and the Son, whosoever denieth the Son,
the same has not the Father. He that
confesseth the Son hath the Father also.

John 4:1 states:

And every spirit that dissolveth Jesus
is not of God. And this is the Antichrist,
of whom you have heard he cometh: and
he is now already in the world.

In this age of evil running rampant, just because this man, this World Teacher, calls himself God does not mean that he is necessarily the Antichrist. It certainly does not mean he is God. With the abundance of cult leaders claiming they too are God, we have to prove other criteria.

The Antichrist has got to be a power broker in order to pull the world leaders together. He is not some delusional cult leader. The World Teacher has already clearly shown his leadership capabilities. Beyond that, he has what best could be described as extraordinary "powers." There have been verified "miracles" around the globe attributed to him.

A most curious point was brought up during my interview with the World Teacher's aide. The aide claimed that the World Teacher had focused his attention on Princess Diana and had communicated to her the need for her philanthropic work. This was not only with AIDS patients but it entailed her campaign for the removal of land mines. This aide attests to the fact the World Teacher generated power in Diana and that she became so immensely popular that she eclipsed Prince Charles. He went on to say that the worldwide phenomenal outpouring of grief when she died was because the World Teacher moved the world to display their mourning on such an unprecedented scale.

Granted, Diana was a big hit and the supposed Antichrist may just be taking credit for her huge drawing power in a star-crazed society. For the sake of argument, though, if this man really has this motivational power, things could get quite interesting in the near future.

To fulfill the role of the Antichrist, the man must be born a Jew. Apparently, this World Teacher was once a Jew and may have been raised a Catholic. His mother was a Jewish prostitute and his father was a renegade monk. Thus, his background is the absolute negation of Jesus.

The Antichrist is a man of peace, at least in the beginning. The World Teacher has proclaimed that he is the peacemaker sought by the world. Only the contrary is true. Behind the scenes, the Antichrist has been stirring up emotion and hatred whether in Iraq, Kosovo, Pakistan or India. In actuality he has been wooing world leaders into his web and openly discussing peace.

Prophecy speaks about the great betrayal by the Antichrist with the world leaders. He has been promising many things to these leaders, but eventually he intends to kill most of them, thereby throwing more confusion into what will be a chaotic reality for everyone.

On October 1, 1988, Heaven told Veronica Lueken that the United Nations would be destroyed along with many of the world's leaders.

> *I see murder ahead now, My child,*
> *in your city of New York. Many shall*
> *be mowed down. It is an attack by a*
> *communist nation.... It is their object*
> *to destroy all and cause chaos in the*
> *city of New York. With their plans there*
> *will be bombs placed in strategic places*
> *and many shall die at the hands of these*
> *ruffians.*

One American seer believes that an assassin will kill these leaders inside a conference room at the United Nations. There may even be nuclear weapons used to destroy the United Nations and New York City.

According to another visionary, this meeting is totally the Antichrist's idea. He will tell the world leaders when to meet, even suggesting he will be there, but he won't show up, nor his close associates. The world leaders will not get the power and money promised them for turning their countries over to the Antichrist's leadership. Instead, they will get death. Another apparent lie in a string of deceptions.

The Antichrist plans on going on worldwide television to take credit for the Warning. Modern day prophets have encouraged God's faithful not to watch this man or listen to him. Even pictures of this man might be harmful. It has been intimated that the pictures might invite his presence. At first, this might seem foolish or superstitious. I assure you it is not.

The man is mesmerizing, literally. One should be extremely careful not to look the Antichrist directly in his eyes. His hypnotic capabilities are beyond anything we have ever experienced in history. We have seen people do evil things, but never in history have we experienced a person totally consumed by evil. Not even Hitler compares to this man. Part of the Antichrist's "army" is beyond our interpretation of evil as well. In fact, they are supposedly out of this world, as we shall see in the next chapter.

All of this build-up will result in a major decision for each us: Do we follow him or reject him? With the scheduled events closing in, we will soon be at the point of no return.

Chapter Eight

UFOs

Everyone has an opinion about UFOs. Either you have seen one or you haven't. Several years ago, I had done extensive research regarding UFOs and the government. To say there has been a cover-up would be a gross understatement. One of the main things I gathered from my investigation was how far the government was willing to go to protect this "secret" which is hardly a secret anymore.

UFO's are spotted everyday. Squadrons of them fly over Mexico City and the video is splashed all over television. Major sightings like the one in Phoenix in 1997 had thousands of witnesses. Personally, I live in a UFO corridor. It is a place where they are somewhat common. Most of the ranchers here have experienced first hand some form of extraterrestrial activity. Those who have not, know people whose cattle have been mutilated.

One night in the summer of 1996, I noticed a bright orange light just above the horizon on our ranch. The evening was clear and visibility was good. There seemed to be a very slight pulsing to the light as it descended over the pasture. The object stayed there for a few minutes, then took off straight up into the air a few feet, then disappeared, almost as if the sky swallowed the object instaneously. No sound accompanied this sighting.

The next morning our mail person came up to the ranch house. She happened to live down the road. So I asked her if she had seen the orange light. She said she wasn't surprised. "Happens all the time out here." I asked her what she thought it was. She said she thought it was a UFO or some government project.

I spent four years digging for answers and asking a lot of questions. In fact, I asked so many questions that I became a pet peeve of the Pentagon. The results of the investigation were quite worthwhile and more than surprising. Even more astonishing was the UFO piece of the prophecy/politics puzzle.

The government has denied the existence of UFO's no matter what the witnesses have said, what radar screens have indicated, what actual photographs, videos or other verifications have shown. Only a handful of government people will go against the grain and call for hearings and investigations. It is obvious that people have been silenced.

There was hope over twenty-five years ago that the government might do something about this phenomenon.

Quoted in the Columbus Citizen Journal in October 18, 1973, United States Representative J. Edward Roush (D-Ind.) said,

> *The increased sightings nationally*
> *could lead to a state of panic and*
> *hysteria and we ought to be concerned*
> *about it.*

Note: this comment taken from the approved text of the Secret of La Sallete from the early 1800's.

For the time has come when the most
astonishing wonders will take place
on the earth and in air... Satan will
have great power over nature: there
will be churches built to serve
these spirits. People will be transported
from one place to another by these evil
spirits...

When I first read that quote it astounded me. These visionaries lived a century before airplanes. It further encouraged me to see if I could find a connection with prophecy and the UFOs. First, you have to see if UFO's really do exist.

A well-documented sighting in Brazil had UFO enthusiasts drooling because it produced an actual "alien." In January of 1996, a town called Varginha, which is approximately two hundred miles northeast of Rio, had an extraordinary experience. Dozens of residents saw a gray, submarine shaped object flying over the city.

Later firemen were called to a wooded area and were reportedly seen walking out of the woods with an extraterrestrial. Following that, three young women on their way home from work reported seeing another alien huddled against a brick wall.

The alien was described as about three feet tall, chocolate skin, no nose or mouth, rubbery limbs, bulging red eyes and three horns protruding from a massive forehead. Also reported by these women was a foul stench secreted by the creature.

Sources reported that the firemen took one of the aliens to military officials at a local army base. Apparently, the creature died a short time later.

These creatures differ greatly from the beings involved in the Roswell crash in 1947. In that crash, the beings were described as gray aliens with large black eyes. Reports indicated that there was one survivor that the Army detained at an undisclosed location. The bodies of his shipmates were shipped back east but there are no records of where the bodies were taken.

So, there is evidence that these visitors are not human in nature nor are the ships piloted by our military as some people have suggested.

Veronica Lueken was told by the Blessed Mother dozens of times about UFOs.

> *You will inform your men of knowledge –*
> *scientists – that the vehicles known as*
> *UFOs are but transports from hell sent to*
> *deceive and confuse mankind and set him in*
> *quest of another world that doesn't exist.*
> (September 13, 1974)

Speaking again about UFOs, Our Lady said to Veronica Lueken on December 31, 1974:

> *They are gathering in great multitudes*
> *upon your weather. Know that they are*
> *of an illusion – a delusion to mankind.*
> *It is but one of the false miracles of*
> *Satan.*

It was just such false miracles that Malachi Martin knew would bring about a great debate over true origins of life. These so-called aliens will supposedly distract us and try to negate the creation of man in the Bible. Precisely, we will hear that these sentient foreign creatures created us and that they "deposited" us on earth thousands of years ago. Father Martin knew the serious consequences of the "alien" arrival.

Father Martin knew that many wonders and so-called miracles would confuse mankind. For instance, the Blessed Mother again told Veronica Lueken:

> *...these demons will promote accidents*
> *that are not accidents.*

A rumor based on statements by pilots regarding recent airline crashes indicate perhaps a foreign object or craft has been be responsible. If this is true, it adds a whole new twist to the terrorist angle.

Israel is worried about just that kind of terrorist attack. In reality, Israel has become a UFO hot spot.

Not only has Israel experienced cattle mutilations, and close encounters of the third kind, but even more ominous, alien abductions. Realizing just how small Israel is, 260 miles long by 70 miles wide at the widest point, scientists are baffled that no other country in the Middle East has this problem.

The sightings of grays in Israel seem to be the norm. According to people who have the dubious fortune of communicating with these beings, all of their discussions are telepathic in nature.

A monumental event happened after a month long series of sightings in Haifa in 1987. As the sightings ended, one spectacular explosion took place at Shikmonah Beach that scorched the sand. The scorch marks were in the shape of a spacecraft. Obviously, someone wanted people to know what had supposedly caused the explosions. Scientists ran tests on the site and found the area to be highly magnetic. The burn site also had a high concentration of zinc.

Still, not one Arab country has the problem. Perhaps, this suggests that this activity is spiritual in nature. It has been suggested in one camp that these might be angels of the Bible who used chariots of fire. On the other side of the argument are the people who believe these aliens are nothing more than demons pretending to be from other civilizations and planets. Many secular scientists back that concept.

Jacques Vallee, a computer scientist and astrophysicist wrote about witness reactions to the aliens in *Dimensions: A Casebook Of Alien Contact*. Vallee believes people view the aliens as demonic due to their "impredictability" and "mischievousness."

A United Nations ambassador along with his colleagues, were purportedly abducted off the Brooklyn Bridge in New York. The ambassador was on his way to the United Nations and was taken right out of his car. From his reactions to the abduction, it was quite clear that his experiences were terrifying and that the creatures exuded evil in their control over him. According to him, it did not matter where they came from, either a distant planet or Hell.

Any valid study into UFO's would have to include findings in Egypt by a group of Egyptologists. Recent discoveries appear to be clues regarding man's origin, confirming what Malachi Martin thought would happen regarding the opening of the pyramids. Father Martin had discussed the similarities of the Sphinx at Giza to what appears to be a face on Mars. He knew that just the suggestion of life from another planet or galaxy would be the beginning of tremendous happenings in the skies.

These celestial events would be used for several purposes. One such purpose is the control of our weather system. It is blatant that our weather patterns have gone crazy. Whether you blame El Nino or La Nina, the effects are still the same: global upheaval, droughts, floods, mud slides and a jet stream with what appears to have a mind of its own.

If you look beyond the bizarre weather patterns and see what is going to happen around the globe, you will see crop failures so huge, the outcome will be disastrous. Obviously, if there isn't any grain or hay for livestock, and no food crops, worldwide famine will quickly follow.

Some scientists believe this is due in part to project HAARP. This multi-billion dollar experiment is located in Gahona, Alaska. HAARP stands for High Frequency Active Auroral Research Project and it is the military's baby. This "baby" is built to alter the ionosphere. Spread over four acres are three hundred and sixty, seventy-two foot tall antennas. These antennas are capable of beaming in excess of one billion watts of radiated power into the Earth's ionosphere.

A Department of Defense document mentioned one of HAARP's applications would "enhance present civilian capabilities" in communications. Previous High Frequency projects were to "gain a better understanding" of the ionosphere, according to the government.

HAARP's mission though differs from the High Frequency Heaters in Puerto Rico and Norway in that its goal is to "perturb" the ionosphere with extremely powerful beams. In essence, the heaters burn holes through the positive and negative charged particles above the earth's surface just to see what happens.

One source close to the project believes weather manipulation, especially over countries not close to the United States, might be one of the chief goals. One such goal would be to disrupt enemy communications and weaponry.

This project could have devastating effects on world weather according to many scientists familiar with the project. Perhaps that is the idea. There may be more to this project than meets the eye. Puerto Rico, home to part of this heater project, has been under investigation by UFO groups. They believe the island is home to a major underground UFO base. Norway as well has been involved in their own highly visible UFO activity.

Project HAARP seems to have had some characteristics of Nikola Tesla's Death Ray. Nikola Tesla was born in Croatia on July 10, 1856. It was apparent very early on that he was quite intelligent. During his early life, Tesla was often ill. He suffered a peculiar malady that caused brilliant flashes of light to appear before his eyes, often accompanied by hallucinations. Tesla believed the visions were linked to his many inventions.

His death ray focused a super powerful thin beam that would not break down over long distances. Tesla promoted this beam that could knock down incoming bombs or attacks. This was in 1908. Interestingly, the Department of Defense has also said this is one of HAARP's capabilities.

When Commander Robert Perry was conducting his second attempt to reach the North Pole, Tesla had notified Perry that he would try to contact them. Perry was in turn to notify Tesla if he noticed anything unusual out on the open tundra.

On June 30, 1908, Tesla aimed his death ray across the Atlantic Ocean towards the North Pole. When Tesla first turned on his machine, he thought it was not working properly. A dim light was the only thing emitted from the device and it was hardly visible. A few minutes later an owl crossed the beam and was disintegrated instantly. That was the end of the test.

Tesla watched the newspapers to see if anything happened and was ready to dub the death ray a failure. However, an article appeared in the paper about a strange thing that happened in Siberia.

A massive explosion had obliterated Tungusha in the remote Siberian wilderness. The date was June 30th. Five hundred thousand square acres of land were wiped out. This explosion was the largest in human history, far surpassing nuclear bombs. Fascinating to note, especially with prophecies of end time comets, that scientists had first reported this explosion as being caused by a mammoth meteorite or comet, but no impact crater was ever found.

Tesla, relieved no one was killed, dismantled the death ray machine. He then turned his attention to the development of technology in Resonance.

Tesla fired up a small oscillator in his New York City Lab, small vibrations occurred in the building. Suddenly, concerned police officers burst into the lab ordering Tesla to turn off the machine. Apparently, Tesla had sent much of Manhattan into tremors.

Moving on, Tesla worked very hard at trying to communicate with alien life forms, convinced that they lived on Mars. He kept up the pursuit until his death. There has been speculation about Tesla and where he got his knowledge. Some felt it might have been alien technology to begin with, while others believed him to consort with the devil.

Immediately following Tesla's death in 1943, his records, blueprints and inventions were confiscated by the government. Tesla had taken technology to the point that it had gone beyond this world. It is plausible to see that domination of the weather and communication controls can be put into practice. These ideas are real and although the intentions behind these practices have been shrouded, evidence has surfaced to give us a glimpse of the why behind the what. The relationship between technology and UFO's has become increasingly clearer. This union is a critical component to our government and the Antichrist.

The Bible tells us about what to expect from the skies in the last days. In Luke, Chapter 21:25-26, it mentions:

> *And there shall be signs in the sun,*
> *and in the moon, and in the stars; and*
> *upon the earth distress of nations, by*
> *reason of the confusion of the roaring*
> *of the sea and of the waves; Men withering*
> *away for fear, and expectation of what*
> *shall come upon the whole world. For the*
> *powers of Heaven shall be moved.*

One thing people forget or do not know is that the Antichrist is extremely well versed in the Bible. He has to be in order to perpetrate the supreme deception of all. The signs in the heavens are to indicate to mankind that the Second Coming of Christ is near.

The Greek word for sign literally means a "supernatural phenomenon intended to point the observer to a profound truth." Christians and Jews are looking for Jesus and these are the groups the Antichrist wants to convince he is the messiah.

As mentioned earlier, according to some prophets, the Antichrist is using UFOs to indoctrinate us into the belief that life began on another planet and that our common perception of God is flawed. The Antichrist will attempt to prove life's origins are far from divine.

During an interview with the Antichrist's promoters, I asked about his connection with the UFOs. The Antichrist's representatives were extremely reluctant to discuss the grays, their ships and their ultimate goal. I was told that these "aliens" are just part of the Messiah and his plans. We should not fear them.

My research has shown that these alien life forms will help the Antichrist orchestrate a false Second Coming, produce wonders in the sky and terrorize the planet.

In pre-Nazi Germany, as Hitler assumed power, he used a consultant well versed in the Apocalypse. This consultant designed Hitler's high energy, hypnotic speeches choreographing every nuance that would cultivate the messiah persona. It was the belief then that the Second Coming had arrived and this time Jesus was a savior with considerable power. Obviously, Hitler was no savior. He couldn't even save himself, but for a time he had many believers. Hitler utilized primitive hologram images of the Virgin Mary and other images to convey a real sense that Judgment was near.

Today, with laser technology and the help of the UFO's, we are set to see some "miraculous" sights, all prepared to convince us that the Antichrist is God.

Michael Brown, author of *The Final Hour*, has done research into UFOs. He believes they are physical manifestation of spiritual phenomenon. Brown writes,

> *We are seeing the actual manifestation*
> *and materialization of forces of good*
> *and evil in direct combat. We're on that*
> *battleground, we're right in the middle*
> *of that crossfire right now.*

Knowing we are right in the thick of things, Heaven is sending us its own wonder that will allow us to see the lines of good and evil more clearly before it is too late. This is a beautiful gift from God, personalized for each one of us. It is a miracle, but more than that. It is *The Miracle.*

Chapter Nine

The Miracle

On a summer evening in 1961, four girls were playing outside the village of Garabandal, Spain. Suddenly, they heard a loud noise, almost like thunder. A luminescent St. Michael the Archangel allegedly appeared to them. The next day he appeared again in the same place and announced they would see the Virgin Mary on July 2nd.

Sunday, July 2, 1961, Conchita Gonzales, Maria Dolores (Mari Loli), Jacinta Gonzales and Mari Cruz returned to the spot where they had met the Archangel. Many people had come into town for the weekend, including physicians and priests. It was 6:00 p.m.

The girls immediately went into ecstasy. Our Lady appeared to the girls along with two angels, one of whom was St. Michael.

There were many more apparitions after this. Between 1961 and 1962, Our Lady appeared to girls several times a week. At the beginning of the apparitions, the girls would immediately fall to their knees. Often, they would strike sharp rocks with a loud noise, but no injuries were ever present. Witnesses have reported that the expressions on their faces were instantly transformed. The girls became unusually beautiful. People said that there was no adequate way to describe the beauty and wonder of their appearances.

During these ecstasies, the girls could not be distracted or disturbed in any way. They displayed no reaction to pin pricks or burns. There was not one attempt of distraction that succeeded.

Doctors even shined bright lights directly in the pupils, but their eyes did not even flicker. In fact, the girls never blinked. Their faces and eyes showed incomparable joy. Yet, when the girls returned to their normal state, they would protect their eyes from the harsh lights.

These ecstasies would last from a few minutes to several hours. Often, the girls would be in awkward positions, at times being totally off balance. Yet, the girls never fell.

Many visitors joined the Garabandal locals at the apparitions. The people would bring objects such as medals and rosaries to be kissed by Our Lady. The girls would raise them up to the Blessed Mother and she would kiss them. Then the Blessed Mother guided the girls in returning the articles back to their owners. All of this was done while the girls were still in ecstasy. Often, the visitors would give their rosaries or medals to another person to be kissed, but when the things were returned, they were given back to the original owners.

At times, some of the items kissed by Our Lady emitted a fragrance like roses. According to Conchita, objects kissed by the Blessed Mother would have miracles from Jesus worked through them.

Not long after the first appearance of Our Lady, the ecstatic walks started. While in ecstasy the four girls would walk throughout the village. They would go up and down stairs, in and out of homes, either day or night. I have seen video of their walks. It is hard to describe. The girls could go backwards and forwards, running or walking. They never fell or tripped. Constantly, their eyes were apparently focused on the Blessed Mother. Viewing the tape gave me the sense that these girls were really in ecstasy. There was no other explanation for their incredible behavior.

An angel told Conchita that God would perform a miracle so that all the people would believe in the apparitions. She would receive a miraculous communion and the Host would appear on her tongue for the people to see it. Up to this time, the girls had appeared to be receiving communion, but no Hosts were visible to the crowd. This time would be different.

Conchita would have fifteen days before the miracle and she informed the public. On July 18, 1962, Garabandal was packed with visitors. Around midnight, Conchita left her house with the visitors who were in her home and went out into the street. She walked a short distance from her house, and then fell to her knees in ecstasy surrounded by the crowd. Lanterns were lifted up to her face. Conchita put out her tongue as if to receive communion. There was nothing on her tongue. In a few moments, witnesses saw a white Host appear on her tongue. Don Alezandro Damians, a businessman from Barcelona, captured this on film. Damians was less than three feet from Conchita. The footage is incredible and it is easy to see the Host appear on Conchita's tongue. A picture of this miracle is provided in the picture section of this book.

This miracle provided confirmation that mystical events were indeed happening in the pines at Garabandal.

The girls had been told several things would occur in the future. The first such occurrence would be that of the Warning. According to the Blessed Mother, after the Warning, the world will be in need of a great miracle.

The Miracle will occur on a Thursday evening at 8:30 p.m. on the feast day of a Eucharistic martyr in March, April or May. The miracle will last approximately fifteen minutes. Supposedly, it will coincide with a great event in the Church.

Many cures will take place for those who go to Garabandal and many unbelievers will convert. According to Conchita, a permanent sign will be left at the Pines as proof of Our Lady's love for all of us.

This "sign" will be seen, photographed and televised, but it will not be able to be touched. It will appear clearly that it is something not of this world but of God.

Conchita has been given permission by Our Lady to announce the date of the miracle eight days in advance. This miracle will be of the utmost importance for everyone. One priest, Father Luis Marie Andreu, was given a view of the Miracle. He was so amazed at the content and the love he felt from God, that he died of happiness that very night. Father Andreu was thirty-eight and in perfect health.

This miracle of love will be our final warning, our final outreach from God who will tell us we are due for a monumental punishment. With this Miracle it will be evident who God is, how much He loves us, and that we must make our final choice – God or the Antichrist.

Although the nature of the miracle was not disclosed at Garabandal, other visionaries have been told about it in visions or locutions.

One such visionary described the Miracle as a brilliant pillar of light. In that light we will see the deceased members of our families in heaven. These relatives will be able to speak to us for a brief time. We will be aware of what is good and what is evil. It will be clear there is a God, and conversely, there is Lucifer.

This visionary also reported that it was made known that you do not have to be in Garabandal in order to witness it. Television will broadcast the Miracle and it will be visible at apparition sites around the world. It is also felt, though, that we all will see it wherever we are, much like the Warning.

Cures will also happen, whether you are at Garabandal or not. Apparently, there is a reason for these cures apart from the mercy and love of God. According to some visionaries, it is so we will be able to make a clear choice for God or the Antichrist without the burden of illness clouding our thoughts. Conversions will also take place across the globe along with the physical cures.

There is one person who is waiting in joy-filled hope for the Miracle. This man will be absolute testimony to the power of God and His generosity in giving to mankind such a precious gift in the Miracle.

His name is Joey Lomangino from Brooklyn, New York. Born into an Italian-immigrant family in 1930, Joey did all he could growing up to help support his family. The oldest of five sons, Joey went to work after school with his dad who had an ice and coal route.

One day when he was sixteen, Joey went to pick up the coal truck for his father. Noticing one of the back tires was low; he took off the tire and rolled it to a gas station six blocks away.

Joey recalls, "I had both knees on top of the tire. I was checking the air pressure and looking at the tire."

His father, Charlie, heard the explosion from around the corner but did not pay much attention. The tire Joey had been kneeling on exploded directly into his face.

Taken to the hospital, Joey was in a coma. The bones in his lower forehead were crushed. A three-inch fracture between the eyes severed his olfactory and optic nerves. For three weeks, Joey laid in that coma until finally waking to the dark world he has known ever since.

After Joey's accident, the family faced poverty. With the stress of Joey's disability, Charlie's health declined and he was no longer able to run his business. He finally found work as a long shoreman but only brought home twelve hundred dollars a year, hardly enough to support a large family. Consequently, the family was destitute. Joey had been on the verge of having the ice and coal business flourish and then the accident happened. It left him profoundly saddened.

Not finding much solace in religion, Joey said,

I wasn't sold on God because I
didn't understand why people suffered.
My parents were good people and they
suffered a lot. This was a sad mystery
I accepted without anger but without
trying to understand either.

Joey worked hard and managed to receive his high school diploma. Things then began to change for him. A businessman loaned Joey money to take over a failing sanitation business. He turned the business into a moneymaker within a year.

However, Joey nearly worked himself into the ground. His doctor ordered him to take a trip, so he went to visit his uncle in Bari, Italy. One day his uncle suggested that they take a seventy-mile trip to San Giovanni Rotundo where Joey would meet the stigmatist priest, Padre Pio. At his uncle's insistence, Joey attended 5:00 a.m. Mass celebrated by the holy priest. After mass, Joey knelt with hundreds of others to receive Padre Pio's blessing. When Padre Pio got to Joey, he called him by name, tucked him on the cheek and then blessed him.

Joey returned to the United States but he never got Padre Pio out of his mind. He even left an opening for God, but this was just the beginning. Still, he did not attend mass regularly and had not really changed his life. Joey continued to be financially successful in his business, but for the most part was unhappy.

Feeling empty, Joey decided to return to San Giovanni Rotundo to see Padre Pio. While he was there, Joey went to confession with Padre Pio. Joey knelt beside the priest who grabbed Joey's wrist and said, "Joey, confess yourself." Shocked at being face to face with Padre Pio, Joey couldn't speak.

Padre Pio said again, "Joey, confess yourself." Joey searched for the words to tell the priest, but when they did not come, Padre Pio spoke up. The priest began to tell him in English all the sins Joey had committed.

Joey remembers that,

> *Padre Pio said, "Joey, do you recall*
> *one night in a bar, a girl named Barbara,*
> *the sin you committed?" I said yes, Padre,*
> *I do, and then he went down the list of*
> *my sins I had committed and the places*
> *I was at.*

Padre Pio finished the list of sins and then asked Joey if he was sorry for having committed them. Joey said he was. Then something sensational happened. According to Joey,

> *Padre Pio raised his hand in the*
> *air and said, "I call Jesus and Mary*
> *for you." I said, "For me? You call*
> *Jesus and Mary for me? He said, "Si."*
> *As Padre Pio gave me absolution, my*
> *eyes [what was left of them] rolled*
> *in my head. I started to rub my face,*
> *my head kept going around and around.*
> *I felt something was happening to me*
> *but I didn't know what it was.*

Joey continued,

> *All of a sudden, my head cleared. Then*
> *Padre Pio touched my lips, made me kiss*
> *the wound on his hand, gave me a tap*
> *on the face and said, "Joey, a little*
> *patience, a little courage and you're*
> *going to be alright.*

From that moment on, Joey's life changed. He now viewed his blindness only as an inconvenience. His renewed faith made him feel like a kid again.

A few days later, Joey knelt with fifty other men waiting for Padre Pio to pass by at the monastery. Suddenly, Joey flung his arms up to protect himself from what he thought was an explosion. It was actually the scent of roses. For years Joey had not been able to smell and the shock of the scent was like an explosion to him. Padre Pio touched Joey on the bridge of his nose and told him not to be afraid. Joey regained his sense of smell against all medical hope.

A friend had accompanied Joey to Italy on the condition that the men journey to Garabandal after leaving Italy. Joey did not know much about Garabandal and only wanted to stay with Padre Pio. He wanted to find out from Padre Pio if the apparitions at Garabandal were real. Looking for a way not to have to go to Garabandal, Joey was hoping for a negative response from the priest.

Joey asked Padre Pio if it was true that the Virgin Mary was appearing to four girls in Garabandal. Padre Pio answered, "Yes." At this point Joey was still reluctant about the trip so he asked Padre Pio if they should go there and the priest said, "Yes, why not?"

So Joey and his friend went to Garabandal and met the visionaries. The men were impressed with the girls' simplicity, their honesty and their devotion to their prayer life. Joey was quite moved with what was happening on that mountain in Spain. Before he left for the United States, Conchita gave him a rosary kissed by the Blessed Mother.

After arriving back home, Joey felt he had to do something to spread the message of Garabandal, especially the news of the Warning. So, Joey decided to go house to house telling the story of Garabandal. He also had wonderful news that he wanted to share about the Miracle and what Conchita had written to him.

Conchita wrote:

Dear Joey: Today at the pines in
a locution, the Blessed Virgin told

me to tell you, you will receive
new eyes on the day of the Great
Miracle...

With that impetus, Joey Lomangino started his worldwide organization dedicated to the Blessed Mother and Garabandal. His healing will truly be a testimony to the veracity of these visions. This man's eyes, totally destroyed, will be completely replaced. Joey knows that is true affirmation about the power of God and something science will not be able to explain.

The timing of the miracle will be most interesting. It will come at a time when we will be approaching a crossroads. The presence of the Antichrist will be more overwhelming and after the Miracle will overpower humanity. He will make massive changes in our lives, forced changes with heavy consequences.

When we experience the Miracle, we will be marked either for God or the Antichrist. The manic Antichrist will constrain the world by his mark, his bar code and/or his computer chip. Although, immediately preceding the Warning and for a short time after, our lives will be difficult. However, they will be manageable with planning and a major change in priorities. We will experience different needs than we in America have ever experienced.

As the powers of good and evil come out of their respective corners after the Miracle, all bets will be off. The horrors we will experience will drive many over the edge unless we focus on God. The Antichrist will do everything he can to destroy the pillar of light that will be left at Garabandal, eventually using nuclear weapons against it, but to no avail.

Madness, his madness, will permeate the earth, as the next chapter will discuss.

Chapter Ten

The Mark Of The Beast

A research group of over one hundred scientists from all over the United States had a joint project in 1968: to invent and develop a microchip that could be imbedded under the skin, but it had to have the ability to identify the person who had it implanted. Further, the person wearing the chip must be able to be located. This was a joint venture allegedly funded by General Electric, Motorola and the United States Government.

Dr. Carl Sanders, a PhD in engineering, claimed that he headed the project. He accidentally stumbled onto this plan. Originally, it was a medical problem that the scientists had to solve. The original goal of the scientists was to find a biotech device that would alleviate or adjust functions in the body. One of the first aspects of the project produced the so-called Rambo chip that was designed to amplify adrenaline flow in the body. Another application was engineered to stop estrogen flow in the pituitary gland.

Still another chip was introduced that would produce electricity in strategic places in the body that would result in behavioral changes. This particular goal did not work well, and the project shifted full time to develop and refine the identification chip.

Surprisingly, Dr. Carl Sanders ostensibly met with One-World government architects nearly twenty times to discuss the project. The One World group, which had Henry Kissinger and members of the CIA involved, was quite concerned about the world's population. According to Sanders, they were desperate to find a way to control over five billion people. Sanders was told that you cannot control them if the people cannot be identified. This idea became the initial directive for Sanders and his group.

The group took twenty years to develop a chip so small that it can easily go through a hypodermic needle. Smaller than a grain of rice, the chip is easily injected into the body. With over 250,000 parts, it is a scientific wonder that can be powered by a tiny lithium battery. It seems the scientists thought of everything. The battery can be recharged by a recharging current using body temperature. There are two places in the human body where temperature changes the quickest. One area is in the forehead below the hairline and the other is in the back of the hand. Nearly two thousand years ago, this was prophesied in the book of Apocalypse.

It is difficult to imagine but below is a list of the data this chip can purportedly store.

- Name and Age
- Address
- Picture of the person's face
- Fingerprints
- Occupation
- Family history
- Income tax records

- Social Security Information, your SSN number plus one digit for international identification. (The nation will be divided into ten regions. Ten leaders will work under the Antichrist to govern the areas)
- Status of Social Security benefits, veteran benefits or railroad benefits.

The chip has over 240 functions and has nine categories of information with plenty of room for subcategories. Equipped with a transmitter, the chip emits a destination signal on the L-Band (1000 Mhz). A controller can pick up the signal using a satellite. Believe it or not, the person can be located within ten feet of their actual location. Right now, there are about twenty-five low earth orbiting satellites or LEO's that can decipher and read a postage stamp lying on the ground. Our license plates can be read every nineteen minutes.

Dr. Sanders did find a down side to the chip. Apparently, the problem is with the lithium battery: It causes a boil or sore that does not heal. Sanders sought confirmation with a physician at Boston Medical Center. The doctor confirmed Sander's findings.

Here's what the book of Apocalypse says about the Mark and the resulting sore, found in chapter 16:2

And the first [angel] went and poured out
his bowl upon the earth, and a sore
and grievous wound was made upon the
men who have the mark of the beast,
and upon those who worship his magic.

It has further been supported that we can be screened from home, whatever we do; whatever objects we have in the home such as holy statues or pictures can be seen. Our conversations can be monitored in any room. This of course cannot be achieved by the implants but rather the chips in our television sets or VCR's. According to some scientists, the newer television sets act like an interactive eye, maintaining surveillance as long as the chip is in our home.

The ID chip will be handed out on a large scale, as the Antichrist is more in the public eye. Food will be scarce and money will be worthless.

Rationing will be the norm but black markets will do quite well. That is why it is important to stock up on things that can be used for barter, such as cigarettes, coffee, sugar and toilet paper, to name a few.

The Antichrist will utilize the chip to force people to worship him. All those who do not accept the chip will be captured, imprisoned and tortured. Millions will be killed. Yet, according to the Bible, if we take the Mark, we are destined for hell.

We have already seen the advent of smart cards, a prelude to the implanted chip. Commercials have pushed the use of the cards by suggesting that merchants won't always take a check and that the cards are safer to carry than cash. It looks as if we are one major transaction away from eternity.

Some years after the invention of this chip, Sanders read the book of Apocalypse, particularly Chapter Thirteen. To his amazement and to his horror, he found that this chip was described in the Bible.

Dr. Sanders said he was inspired by God to reveal to the real purpose behind the chip. He refused. Not long after, Sanders was diagnosed as having cancer. His doctors gave him two to six months to live. God was not through with Carl Sanders, however, and He spoke to him again about his decision. God discussed Sanders' disobedience and his obstinacy. Dr. Sanders changed his mind and began to inform the world.

Surviving major surgery, Dr. Sanders became a Christian, proclaiming the wonders of God and the perils of his chip.

Obviously Prince Charles did not hear Dr. Sanders' warnings. His sons, Princes William and Harry purportedly have had the chip imbedded in the event that they are ever kidnapped.

There have been interested groups in the Mark of the Beast who have debunked Carl Sanders and even reported that Sanders had retracted his statements. People have tried to find Sanders, but no one has heard from him.

The United States government has accepted the technology about which Sanders spoke and has been implementing it for troop identification. Metal dog tags are becoming a thing of the past. According to the Department of Defense, PIC's or Personal Identification Carriers are being issued to military personnel. They can hold 256 megabytes of information, including voice data. The Department of Defense also stated that computers could easily update the chips.

Three million animal identification chips have been implanted around the globe and are working as expected. A few medical experts think we are not ready to implant the chips as yet. Lately, however, we have seen chips surgically implanted to assist in vision. So far, the results are remarkable. Blind patients are able to see light and objects and the future looks promising.

Also under development is the programmable tattoo invented by Andrew Singer. This tattoo is considered to be a visible implant, which lies close to the surface of the skin making the display easy to read. Merely holding your wrist or forehead under an external charger keeps the battery fresh. Financial institutions are pushing these implants claiming that cash is obsolete and the risk of theft is negligible.

Bar codes are also another aspect of marking people. Long in practice in retail, the bar code has already debuted as identification for military personnel, prisoners and school children in larger cities. It has been reported that the bar code is capable of containing the whole genetic structure of the person.

Anyone who has traveled to a police state knows the anxiety or the all-out fear that comes with being asked for identification papers by soldiers. Adolph Hitler insisted that all citizens carry their papers in Nazi Germany. Fear was readily instilled by the establishment, especially when pressing citizens on the street for their documents.

The United States government, unlike other countries throughout the world, has met with heavy resistance when it comes to the National Identification Databank. For now the forced national I.D. card has failed to gain momentum. Still, people like Diane Feinstein as early as 1995 pushed Congress into making the National I.D. law.

Riding on the panic train driven by a huge immigration problem in California, Feinstein has been desperate to get the system up. In fact, there are some in Congress that want to see chips or numbers assigned to us at birth.

In messages to Father Gobbi, the Blessed Mother elaborated on the Mark of the Beast:

- *The mark is imprinted on the forehead and on the hand.*
- *The forehead indicated intellect, because the mind is the seat of human reason.*
- *The hand expresses human activity because it is with the hands that man acts and works.*
- *He who allows himself to be signed with the mark on his forehead is led to accept the doctrine of the denial of God, or the rejection of his law, and of atheism which in these times, is more and more diffused and advertised. And thus he is driven to follow the ideologies in mode today and to make himself a propagator of all the errors.*
- *If my Adversary is signing with his mark, all his followers, the time has come when I also, your heavenly leader, am signing with my motherly seal, all those who have consecrated themselves to my Immaculate Heart and have formed part of my army.*

With all the latest electronics you have to wonder whether or not we created our own end-time scenario. For instance, the Bible mentions statues being built which we will be forced to worship. Some theologians think one of the most amazing inventions of late could easily be "transformed" into a true idol.

At the University of Tokyo, engineers have created a robot, which looks remarkably human. It has synthetic skin and a neural network that allows it to display five various moods. Cameras will be installed behind its eyes capable of recognizing human expressions. This will allow it to respond to those cues.

Also in Tokyo is a robot built to resemble a Buddhist priest. The robot's eyes blink and his mouth moves. This lifelike robot is located at Yokohama Chuo cemetery in Tokyo. Everyday the robot chants the prayers along with the monks.

Perhaps it is easier to understand how the entire world will be deluded and follow the Antichrist. With the latest technological wonders, he is capable of "creating" quite a show and unfortunately, a lasting impression.

Another weak area where the Antichrist will have a huge impact is in the global financial markets. It is this impact that will effectively close the airtight lid on society. That lid will stay shut until the world capitulates.

With the tremendous difficulties experienced by the Asian Markets in the past few years coupled with the serious decline of their export markets, we find that this is the compound interest on the principal of the collapsing Japanese banking system. This collapse has magnified and exacerbated the economic situation in Asia. The rest of the world is in danger of contamination.

Allan Greenspan said in 1998 at his testimony before the Senate Committee on the Budget that, "It is just not credible that the United States, or for that matter Europe, can remain an oasis of prosperity unaffected by a world that is experiencing greatly increased stress."

Even though Russia is not a significant world trader, its deepening financial woes will never the less further open the dam of instability.

Some analysts in the United States believe we have been thriving in an economic bubble, playing our stock market game under the protection of a dome. With the Dow at an all time high at this writing, and as more investing fans pile into the stadium, the expert Bulls believe we can take the Dow even higher. Additionally, there are the Bears and naysayers who think we will be in for the financial shock wave of all time.

Prophecy seems to give the point spread to the Bears. Although many visionaries agree, the crux of their messages can be summed up in this message given to Veronica Lueken on October 1, 1988:

> *Soon, in the plans of the Eternal*
> *Father, He shall set forth and allow*
> *to come upon mankind a great money*
> *disaster. In this way it will prove*
> *to you that the disaster back in the*
> *1920's, My children, was as nothing*
> *compared to what will happen now. I*
> *talk of a great depression coming*
> *upon mankind. This is well planned*
> *by those in control.*

I am not sure there is much we can do to prevent the coming collapse. Possibly it can be delayed by less leverage on the part of banks with a decrease in debts with added equity.

In any event, we need to remember that the Antichrist does not have that much power. He must rely on tools of deception in order for his plans to work. However, it is encouraging that his reign will be somewhat short-lived. Some of us will be able to miss most of the terrors of this dark time because of the Rapture. Two will be in the field and one will be taken. Two will be in a bed and one will be taken. Which one will you be?

Chapter Eleven

The Rapture

What would you do if half of the population of the world suddenly disappeared? This disappearance is not the result of some nuclear blast but, rather, the hotly contested Rapture. Some people believe in a pre-tribulation rapture, others believe in a post-tribulation rapture, while a great number of people either do not believe or know anything about it.

At least there is some common ground between the pre-Tribulation and the post-Tribulation sides. That is in the definition of what it is and how it will occur. The rapture can be compared to playing the cymbals: It's not how but when.

The word rapture is from the Latin word *rapio*. *Rapio* means, "a snatching away." Christians believe that God's chosen will be snatched up, body and soul, to be with Him in heaven while the rest of the world endures the tribulation and the final chastisements.

It is comforting to think we will not have to experience the trauma that will swallow everyone and everything on earth. Or will we? How do we qualify for this heavenly escape?

The answer depends entirely on whether you answer that question from the Protestant or Catholic perspective.

First, let us look at the supporting text in the Bible that confirms the rapture is something tangible.

We can examine Our Lord's words in St. Luke 17:34-37:

> *I say to you, in that night there*
> *shall be two in a bed; the one*
> *shall be taken, and the other shall*
> *be left. Two women shall be grinding*
> *together; the one shall be taken and*
> *the other shall be left: two men shall*
> *be in the field, the one shall be taken,*
> *and the other shall be left. They answering,*
> *say to him: Where Lord? Who said to them:*
> *Wheresoever the body shall be, thither*
> *will the eagles also be gathered together.*

Some scholars believe as much as fifty percent of the faithful will be raptured and the balance will have to go through the Tribulation. Here is a point where Catholics and Protestants are at odds. To be more specific, I should say Catholics who believe in the Rapture are in disagreement with Protestants regarding the percentages of those people who will be raptured.

Catholics who believe in the Rapture, and they are probably in the minority, also believe and support Church doctrine regarding Purgatory. Purgatory is the place where souls go who have sinned throughout their earthly life, but still did not deserve Hell. Nor did they immediately deserve heaven. Although Catholics believe in God's forgiveness in the sacrament of penance, there is also the belief that the soul is stained. Whereas confession removes the bulk of the stains, there are still the gray spots or blemishes that need to be treated before the soul can go to Heaven. It is similar to the final rinse cycle.

There are other reasons that a soul goes to Purgatory. Little vices or imperfections that need work merit purgatorial suffering. The amount of time a soul needs in Purgatory or the suffering one has to do there is dependent on how we live our lives. Catholics do not believe heaven is directly attainable after death simply because Jesus died on the cross for all sinners. A Catholic believes you need more than a profession that Jesus is the Savior. For instance, Catholics do not believe you can live a sinful life while claiming Jesus and still be allowed heaven.

Some Protestants disagree sharply with this, whether they are pre-Tribulation or post-Tribulation. They feel you do not have to be completely free from sin to go to Heaven and for the focus of this chapter, to be raptured.

One Catholic visionary describes the qualifications for the Rapture in this context. In order to be raptured, a person must have completed their penance for their sins or have completed their purgatorial suffering on earth before the Great Chastisement.

To make more sense of Purgatory, I will explain it this way. If you commit a mortal sin, for instance, sex before marriage, you receive seven years for each time you had intercourse outside of marriage. So, if you confess the sins, do your penance prescribed by the priest, you still have seven years for each offense to "work-off."

This "working-off" or suffering can be done on this side of the grave by offering up ill health, disappointments, making sacrifices (i.e.: giving up certain foods you enjoy, and so forth.) Prayers and charitable acts also expiate the number of purgatorial years.

At Fatima, Lucy asked the Blessed Mother if one of her friends who had died went to Heaven. Our Lady told Lucy that her friend went to Purgatory until the end of time.

Protestants believe *all* men believing in Jesus will be saved and caught up in the 'twinkling of an eye.' They believe the only way a person can be worthy or perfect to stand in front of God is to be washed in His blood and that is the only merit we need. Of course, if you continue to sin, are you truly professing that you are washed in His blood? Protestants do believe that true salvation means your life reflects your conversion. Further, then, they believe that any believer is a member of the Body of Christ and since dismemberment is not possible, then we will all go to the Rapture.

That is a consoling thought but if that isn't true, and the Catholic interpretation is correct, I am sure the swells of "Oops" will be heard around the world! In any case, we should be prepared.

Although no one has an exact date on the Rapture because there seems to be no specific "sign" mentioned, the nature of it has been revealed to several true seers. These seers have gone on the record about the Rapture stating that it will begin after the Miracle and continue right up until the Three Days of Darkness. This also differs with the Protestant belief that it is a one-time occurrence.

You can't help but wonder if the UFO's will be thought to be involved in the rapture. The Blessed Mother said this to Veronica Lueken:

> ...*Many of your news medias shall*
> *state that they have been carried*
> *off by flying saucers.*

Our Lady went on to tell Veronica that the raptured are carried off into a supernatural realm of the Eternal Father to await the return of Jesus to earth.

However, we will have struggles with wickedness in high places. It says this in Ephesians 6:12:

> *For our wrestling is not against*
> *flesh and blood; but against the*
> *principalities and powers, against*
> *the rulers of this world of darkness,*
> *against the spirits of wickedness in*
> *high places.*

According to the Book of Apocalypse Chapter 12:12, they (demons) will be cast to earth. Perhaps with the great number of UFOs due to be seen, this explanation is understandable.

Elias was taken up alive to Heaven as the Bible mentions in 4 Kings 2:11:

> *And as they went on, walking and*
> *talking together, behold a fiery*
> *chariot, and fiery horses parted*
> *them both asunder and Elias went*
> *up by a whirlwind into Heaven.*

God in his mercy is giving us the Rapture so that we will not have to experience the horrendous events that are due. Some visionaries believe that this Rapture has already begun. They cite the large number of missing children in

this country and worldwide as being raptured. Andrew
Wingate has this to say:

> *A time will come before the worst*
> *chastisement comes and in God's Mercy,*
> *God will protect some of the MOST PURE*
> *before this horrific event. This is*
> *the Rapture.*
>
> *The purest are primarily children (up to*
> *15 years of age) to preserve their innocence*
> *and in God's mercy they will be taken up*
> *body and soul to a "state of rapture" or a*
> *"place of sanction and protection," which I*
> *recognize as paradise. They will then return*
> *for the reign of peace (after the 40 years).*
>
> *The rapture has been occurring for years.*
> *Innocent children (mostly infants) have been*
> *taken up body and soul (disappeared) and await*
> *the finality of the greatest chastisement known*
> *to all of mankind. They will then return*
> *incredibly pure of heart and soul with the*
> *remnant church, the faithful who survived.*
> *The rapture will overlap the reign of the*
> *Antichrist.*
>
> *This is God's Mercy that some innocent*
> *souls will be removed and not be exposed to*
> *such ugliness of the reign of the Antichrist.*
> *God's Mercy will prevent the Antichrist*
> *and his cohorts to molest and use these beautiful*
> *souls for his own diabolical use.*

Wingate's opinions agree with Veronica Lueken. Whether it is accurate cannot be answered before the Rapture. Yet, I do believe that many innocent children will be spared the hideous treatment that will befall all people who refuse the Mark of the Beast.

After a great deal of examination of the Rapture, I believe we will see a worldwide panic when people just "disappear." Literally at the time of the rapture, people will just cease to be here. Faster than they can blink, people engaged in conversation, lovemaking, eating, whatever, will be gone.

Certainly, there is a sense that those of us who remain will grow quite fearful at the prospect of having to deal with the end-times on our own. I believe this will be a difficult situation and that, unless we are prepared, unless we know what is going on, we could easily accept the Mark of the Beast, thinking, however falsely, we will find security.

We have already seen particular cults or groups rushing the end-times by creating situations to ensure military conflict between the major countries involved in the Apocalypse. There are other groups such as the Heaven's Gate followers, who dabbled in prophecy, added UFO's, a dash of the Apocalypse, shook, then slipped themselves an eternal mickey.

The closer we come to realizing the seriousness of our times and that it is more supernatural than we dare contemplate, the more we will see what groups are scripting the final days of the era. Knee-jerk reactions on the part of governments will further fan the fires of desperation.

Therefore, it is critical that we do not put all our trust in the rapture to help us escape the unthinkable inevitability. Rather, we should as Padre Pio said, "Pray, hope and don't worry."

As an offering of consolation, the Blessed Mother told Veronica Lueken this:

Those who remain close to My Son
and remain well of spirit will have
no fear for the days ahead. All that
is rotten will fall, and your world
will emerge cleansed and triumphant
in the eyes of God...

With all that is happening around us, the links of prophecy and politics all indicate the rapture could happen at any time. Over three hundred years ago, Sir Isaac Newton went way beyond the principals of gravity and put much of his time into studying and interpreting the Book of Daniel. Newton would have made the top ten list of geniuses without a doubt. So, his findings and calculations for the end days should be of particular interest.

The father of modern science and the industrial revolution was a devout Christian and Bible scholar. Newton was fluent in ancient languages and actually translated the Book of Daniel directly from the Hebrew.

His interpretation of Daniel, Chapter Nine, was basically quite different from everyone else's. For those not familiar with Daniel and his writings, it is believed that God gave Daniel a view of history from his time until the end of history.

Below is the chapter and verse in dispute, which discusses Christ's Second Coming.

Know thou therefore, and take notice: that
from the going forth of the word, to build
up Jerusalem again, unto Christ the prince,
there shall be seven weeks, and sixty two
weeks: and the streets shall be built
again, and the walls in straitness
of times. (Dan. 9:25)

Without getting into a Biblical debate at this point, Newton's view of the timing will be presented. It was Newton's belief that the sixty-two weeks or the 434 years was fulfilled at the First Coming. The "seven" weeks or 49 years refers to the Second Coming of Christ.

The interpretation Newton applied to this verse was that Israel would be born again, predicting a "friendly kingdom" that again would help establish Israel as a country. At the time Newton discussed this, it was too bizarre to take seriously. However the United Nations, acting perhaps as a "friendly kingdom" paved the way for Israel's rebirth in 1947. The Israeli Proclamation of Independence came on May 14, 1948.

These dates are of particular interest to those trying to calculate first the rapture, and then the Second Coming.

Newton's idea of weeks was linked to what he considered the periods of Jewish "Sabbath." Weeks or seven-year periods counted from the Jews entering the land.

According to Newton's understanding, we only have to count these seven weeks from Israel's birth year of 1948 to determine the "approximate" date of Christ's return and from these extrapolate the "approximate" date of the rapture.

Using Israel's rebirth in 1948, or the "entering of the land," you can start the seven-year count on 1948 or 1949. The first "land Sabbath" year in 1954 or 1955 would initiate the countdown ending at 2003 or 2004.

These dates 2003 and 2004 could signal Christ's return. Some Bible scholars believe the dates are more likely to be 2004 or 2005. Although this calculation depends not only on Newton's understanding of the Jewish calendar but also for Biblical scholars, it does show that we are indeed within the rapture time frame.

Nostradamus coincidentally saw 2005 as the date we would be in the thick of it, believing that year 2000 was not as ominous as many prophecies might suggest.

Israel is the key in all of God's prophecies. It is also God's time clock. As to how long the clock will keep ticking is really only known to God. Yet, with the Tribulation soon upon us, I think we will be too busy to check the time.

Chapter Twelve

The Camps

Since the 1950s, when we mention the word "camp" we tend to think about where our children spend time in the summer. When it comes to internment camps, we usually focus on the death camps of World War II. However, the internment camps discussed in this chapter are not the ones in Nazi Germany, but, rather, the ones here in the United States. Speculation and rumor abound in this area fostering great conversation on the airwaves and over the Internet.

Much of the rumors were quelled when more than one official in the government confirmed their existence. However, if you broach the subject at dinner parties, informing your friends about Congressman Henry Gonzales' admission that the camps are real, they look at you as if you were behind a right-wing conspiracy. They usually change their tune and the expressions on their faces when you also inform them the United States Army has acknowledged there are camps all over the country.

After the nervous laughter is out of the way, the first question asked is usually, "For whom are the camps built?" Indigestion inevitably ensues when I answer, "You and me." I don't need to mention that the dinner invitations got fewer and far between with some friends.

The concept of internment camps in the 20th century was implemented in the 1930s. The camps were woven into National security planning or, in the case of Nazi Germany, the Soviet Union and the United States they were actually put into use.

In March of 1933, Hitler opened Dachau and he quickly filled it with thousands of his fellow citizens. Stalin was busy at this time with his "rural collectivization" program. Seven to ten million people were exterminated there and during 1934 to 1939, another ten million people were slaughtered.

Franklin Roosevelt met with J. Edgar Hoover in August of 1939 to discuss and develop a plan for camps in the United States. Auschwitz opened five months later. Of course, it is common knowledge about the detention camps that housed American citizens of Japanese descent during WWII. Once the war ended, America thought it was past this embarrassment.

Moreover, Hoover met with Attorney General J. Howard McGrath in the summer of 1948 to devise a plan that would allow President Truman the power to suspend constitutional liberties during a national emergency. The code name of the project was Security Portfolio and, when in place, it would empower the FBI to arrest up to twenty thousand people and throw them into various security detention centers. Once imprisoned, the prisoners would not have the right to a trial or habeas corpus appeal. Further, the FBI was given the go ahead to create a "watch list" of the people who would be detained. This list contained personal statistics on individuals such as physical description, work address and detailed classifications of their families.

Congress did approve the Internal Security Act in 1950, which contained provisions authorizing an emergency detention plan. Hoover was not satisfied with this Act because it guaranteed the right to a court hearing or habeas corpus. The one aspect Hoover sought was the total suspension of the Constitution.

The FBI, over the course of the next two years, established detention camps and designed seizure plans for thousands of United States citizens. Hoover was still in a tirade and hounded Attorney General McGrath to ignore the provisions in the 1950 Act and give the FBI "official" permission to use the more vicious 1948 plan. In November of 1952, McGrath gave into Hoover's demands.

Congress repealed the Emergency Detention Act of 1950 in 1971. The supposed threat of civilian camps was over, at least on paper. Hearings were held in the senate in 1975 to discuss the fact that the internment camps were still in operation and were never terminated. The Intelligence Activities Senate Resolution 21 revealed a sinister agenda, which detailed plans by the federal government to monitor, arrest, and ultimately imprison large segments of the American population.

Now, it could be argued that the reason this plan was first implemented in 1950 was to address the concerns of Communist infiltration. On the surface, it smacked of McCarthyism. That would not explain the fact that the plan was operating and still expanding in 1975.

The Senate investigation revealed the existence of Master Search Warrant (MSW) and the Master Arrest Warrant (MAW) still in use today. With the MAW, the United States Attorney General can order the FBI to arrest anyone the Attorney General finds dangerous to public place and safety. The person can be detained until further ordered.

The MSW gives the FBI the power to search premises where it is believed that contraband, or other materials (this can mean more than 30 days of food storage) that may be in violation of the Proclamation of the President of the United States. Other items on the list allegedly include:

- firearms
- short-wave radio receiving sets
- cameras
- propaganda
- printing presses

An offspring of the 1975 Senate hearing was the massive database housing names of millions of Americans who have no idea about the existence of the database or the government's interest in them.

President Reagan directed Oliver North and Robert McFarlane in 1982 under National Security Direction 58, to use the National Security Council to secretly retrofit FEMA (Federal Emergency Management Agency) to manage the country in times of national crisis. Under the 1984 REX exercises, a contingency plan was set up for the imprisonment of some 400,000 people. This involved a "simulation" of civil unrest during a national emergency.

This exercise was so secretive, that well-tenured employees were denied access to FEMA's fifth floor. In fact, special heavy-duty doors were installed to keep people out.

It was suggested at the time this was an exercise to handle Central American refugees in case of a war, but the reality was it was designed for American citizens.

The camps set-up under the Rex 84 Exercise are:

- Ft. Chaffee, Arkansas
- Ft. Drum, New York
- Ft. Indian Gap, Pennsylvania
- Camp A. P. Hill, Virginia
- Eglin Air Force Base, Florida
- Vandenberg AFB, California
- Ft. McCoy, Wisconsin
- Ft. Benning, Georgia
- Ft. Huachucha, Arizona
- Camp Krome, Florida

The record clearly indicates that detention centers are here in the United States and they are multiplying every year. It is currently estimated that there are over one hundred internment camps across the country. Although not every state has a camp, every newly demarked section of the country has several. States' jurisdiction and boundaries have very little meaning as far as the government is concerned. On the surface, the government deals directly with the fifty states. Unknown to most the country was divided into ten regions by President Nixon in 1969. Under the Government Reorganization Act, these regions were to be directed by individuals appointed by the president.

Each region would have what is called a Federal Regional Council. One person would be appointed by the President to chair each council. Since then, these ten regions have now been incorporated under FEMA. The map explaining these regions is located in the picture section of this book.

The ten regions are defined as follows:

- *Region One*: Connecticut, Massachusetts, New Hampshire, Rhode Island, Vermont. Regional Capitol: Boston

- *Region Two*: New York, New Jersey, Puerto Rico, Virgin Islands. Regional Capitol: New York City.

- *Region Three*: Delaware, Maryland, Pennsylvania, Virginia, District of Columbia. Regional Capitol: Philadelphia.

- *Region Four*: Alabama, Florida, Georgia, Kentucky, Mississippi, North Carolina, Tennessee. Regional Capitol: Atlanta

- *Region Five*: Illinois, Indiana, Michigan, Minnesota, Ohio, Wisconsin. Regional Capitol: Chicago.

- *Region Six*: Arkansas, Louisiana, New Mexico, Oklahoma, Texas. Regional Capitol: Dallas-Fort Worth.

- *Region Seven*: Iowa, Kansas, Missouri, Nebraska. Regional Capitol: Kansas City

- *Region Eight*: Colorado, Montana, North Dakota, South Dakota, Utah, Wyoming. Regional Capitol: Denver.

- *Region Nine*: Arizona, California, Hawaii, Nevada. Regional Capitol: San Francisco.

- *Region Ten*: Alaska, Oregon, Washington, Idaho. Regional Capitol: Seattle.

Supposedly, these regions were set up to manage the country in case of emergency, usurping states' rights and the ability of state government to govern its own people. Apparently, there have been sweeping changes made, which are unconstitutional and of which people have little knowledge.

FEMA did have the power under the Federal Register, which allowed it to operate existing bureaucratic departments together with regional governments to manage the United States.

Everything changed in 1994. President Clinton issued Executive Order 12919, transferring all Executive Orders authority to the President's Security Advisor. The importance of this order will be shown and what impact it will have on us.

First, Executive Orders become law if not voided by Congress within sixty days. To this point, Congress has yet to repeal any Executive Order.

Here is a list of Executive Orders that recent presidents have issued that are reported to deal with this topic:

10995 – All communications media seized by the Federal Government.

10997 – Seizure of all electrical power, fuels, including gasoline and minerals.

10998 – Seizure of all food resources, farms and farm equipment.

10999 – Seizure of all kinds of transportation, including personal cars, and control of all highways and seaports.

11000 – Seizure of all civilians for work under Federal Supervision.

11001 – Federal takeover of all health, education and welfare.

11002 – Postmaster General empowered to register every man, woman and child in the United States.

11003 – Seizure of all aircraft and airports by Federal Government.

11004 – Housing and finance authority may shift population from one locality to another. Complete integration.

11005 – Seizure of all railroads, inland waterways and storage facilities.

11051 – The Director of the Office of Emergency Planning authorized to put Executive Orders into effect in "times of increased international tension or financial crisis." He is also to perform such additional functions as the President may direct.

It is obvious these orders had very specific purposes in mind as well as specific results. Undoubtedly, it is not to maintain the constitutional rights of Americans.

Several years ago, I did not think my research into prison camps would amount to anything. I thought that they were imaginings of right-winged groups. The records were found and the pictures of these camps do exist.

As I mentioned earlier, these camps are all over the country with the largest camp located in Alaska. Most of these camps are built to house approximately twenty thousand people, while the camp in Alaska can arguably support five hundred thousand. Although there are estimates as low as two hundred thousand. These camps are standing empty right now, but, curiously, the camps have guards on duty.

Some of these facilities are for women only, as in the alleged camp in Wilcox Correctional Institution located in Hawkinsville, Georgia. This facility can house fifteen thousand persons. It, too, is empty but fully manned by guards and staff.

Now, perhaps some food for thought. With dangerous overcrowding in our prison system today, why aren't these new facilities being utilized by the State and Federal Corrections? For the past twelve years, states have come up short with the funding necessary to build enough facilities for the growing prison population. These new prisons are equipped with the latest in security technology, and they sit empty.

Or perhaps a more curious aspect, why have foreign law officers specifically the Hong Kong Royal Police Officers been offered jobs with Federal Law Enforcement?

In recent tests administered to military personnel, Washington found that our troops admitted they would have trouble arresting or incarcerating average Americans. This was a potential problem should the camps be utilized.

Many FBI officials and hundreds of military personnel have taken early retirement rather than be involved with the latest operations. In reality, there is a group of Green Berets who are prepared to fight against any soldiers, foreign or domestic who would try to incarcerate Americans in the camps.

With this type of atmosphere, the FBI and MJTF (Multi Jurisdictional Task Force) have decided to "hire" foreign police, not just any police, but top-notch thugs who would have no problem running the camps.

It has been reported that the government is moving ever closer to the New World Order. Proponents for the Order have come up with what they call C and C. It stands for Capture and Custody.

With C and C in mind, we can look at title 11 of the McCarren Act. Under this act, Operation Dragnet is sanctioned. This operation allows the President of the United States to suspend the Bill of Rights with a single phone call. In the event of invasion, war or insurrection, Operation Dragnet will be implemented. Located at an undisclosed site in Washington, DC, is a computer system, which contains one million names of people who will be immediately exposed to C and C. These names, interestingly enough, are not Islamic terrorists, or foreign spies, but rather American citizens. David Spangler mentioned the reason for this in 1976. Spangler is an influential leader in the push for the New World Order.

In Spangler's book, *Revelation: The Birth Of A New Age*, the author touts all the wonders people will experience with the New World Order. Then Spangler proceeds with a chapter called "Two Worlds" where he explains that people are now divided into two groups: "Those who have raised their consciousness sufficiently to where they can accept the New World Order" and "those who refuse to do so."

The second group, according to Spangler on page 100 of his book, "have no place in the new world." He then goes on to ask two rhetorical questions. "What will happen to those who cannot attune to the new? Where will they go?"

Spangler leaves no doubt in your mind. He says they will be "withdrawn" from the world and sent to "the upstairs room" to be "retrained" in the principals of the New Age. Sounds like the opponents of the New World Order marked for death, just as prophecy has stated. Spangler goes on to drive the point home.

These opponents will stay in their "upstairs room" until they can be safely "released into physical embodiments again," obviously intimating that people will be separated at some point from their earthly vessel. As of yet, Spangler does not have any power, so his threats are relatively benign.

However, if we look at people who do have power, we might be better informed about where the real threats lie.

Louis Gruiffeda, who was head of FEMA ostensibly stated, "Legitimate violence is integral to our form of government, for it is from this source that we can continue to purge our weaknesses."

This is coming from a man who had the "welfare" of citizens as a job description.

Further proof that something sinister is going on, comes from a source close to the White House who has stated, "The President has empanelled a small, trusted group of legal minds...their charge...to identify the options available or needed to extend Clinton's administration beyond its current term..."

The supposed results of this panel were the following points.

Step One: Extend a National State of Emergency as defined under United States Code, Title 50.

Step Two: Cause an event, which is defined under this code (nuclear, biological or chemical weapon threat) the event must be by use of a 'weapon of mass destruction.' The event does not have to happen within the boundaries of the United States.

President Clinton has repeatedly talked about Weapons of Mass Destruction. It is beginning to look like the near future has already been planned.

From the White House Library, we find a press release that is very fascinating.

The White House Office of the Press Secretary
For Immediate Release
November 12, 1997

Notice Continuation Of Emergency Regarding Weapons Of Mass Destruction

On November 14, 1994, by Executive Order 12938, I declared a national emergency with respect to the unusual and extraordinary threat to the national security, foreign policy, and economy of the United States posed by the proliferation of nuclear, biological, and chemical weapons ("weapons of mass destruction") and the means of delivering such weapons.

Because the proliferation of weapons of mass destruction and the means of delivering them continue to pose an unusual and extraordinary threat to the national security, foreign policy, and economy of the United States, the national emergency declared on November 14, 1994, and extended on November 14, 1995 and November 14,1996, must continue in effect beyond November 14, 1997.

Therefore, in accordance with section 202(d) of the National Emergencies Act (50U.S.C. 1622(d)), I am continuing the national emergency declared in Executive Order 12938. This notice shall be published in the Federal Register and transmitted to the Congress.

William J. Clinton
The White House, November 12, 1997

It appears as if all that is needed for the camps to be open for business is an emergency, real or manufactured.

We are moving in a dangerous direction and the people in North America have got to be awakened and readied for what is about to happen.

Chapter Thirteen

The Remnant And The Last Pope

St. Nilus, a fifth century monk, ascetic writer and Bible scholar, had much to say to emperors, rulers and people in power. He was never afraid to tell someone the truth. Many people sought his counsel in all sorts of matters. Nilus was also a prophet and saw what life would be like in our times. The following is one of these prophecies that seem remarkable considering it was written nearly fifteen hundred years ago.

> *After the year 1900, toward the
> middle of the 20th century, the people
> of that time will become unrecognizable.
> When the time for the Advent of the
> Antichrist approaches, people's minds
> will grow cloudy from carnal passions,
> and dishonor and lawlessness will grow
> stronger.*
>
> *Then the world will become
> unrecognizable. People's appearances
> will change, and it will be impossible to*

*distinguish men from women due
to their shamelessness in dress and style
of hair. These people will be cruel and
will be like wild animals because of the
temptations of the Antichrist.*

*There will be no respect for parents
and elders, love will disappear, and
Christian pastors, bishops, and priests
will become vain men, completely failing
to distinguish the right-hand way
from the left. At that time the morals
and traditions of Christians and of
the Church will change. People will
abandon modesty, and dissipation will
reign.*

*Falsehood and greed will attain great
proportions, and woe to those who pile up
treasures. Lust, adultery, homosexuality,
secret deeds and murder will rule in
society. At that future time, due to
the power of such great crimes and
licentiousness, people will be deprived
of the grace of the Holy Spirit, which
they received in Holy Baptism and equally
of remorse.*

*The Churches of God will be deprived of
God-fearing and pious pastors, and woe
to the Christians remaining in the world
at that time; they will completely lose
their faith because they will lack the
opportunity of seeing the light of*

knowledge from anyone at all.

*Then they will separate themselves out of
the world in holy refuges in search of
lightening their spiritual sufferings,
but everywhere they will meet obstacles
and constraints. And all this will result
from the fact that the Antichrist wants
to be Lord over everything and become
the ruler of the whole universe, and he
will produce miracles and fantastic signs.*

*He will also give depraved wisdom to
an unhappy man so that he will discover
a way by which one man can carry on a
conversation with another from one end
of the earth to the other. At that time
men will also fly through the air like
birds and descend to the bottom of the
sea like fish.*

*And when they have achieved all this,
these unhappy people will spend their
lives in comfort without knowing, poor
souls, that it is deceit of the
Antichrist.*

*And, the impious one! -- he will so
complete science with vanity that it
will go off the right path and lead people
to lose faith in the existence of God in
three hypostases.*

*Then the All-good God will see the downfall
of the human race and will shorten the days
for the sake of those few who are being
saved, because the enemy wants to lead
even the chosen into temptation, if that
is possible... then the sword of chastisement
will suddenly appear and kill the perverter
and his servants.*

The children of La Salette were also given this message as it relates to the end-times and the remnant Church.

*I make an urgent appeal to the earth.
I call on the true disciples of the living
God who reigns in Heaven; I call on the
true followers of Christ made man, the
only true Savior of men; I call on my
children, the true faithful, those who
have given themselves to me so that I may
lead them to my Divine Son, those whom I
carry in my arms, so to speak, those who
have lived on my spirit.*

*Finally, I call on the Apostles of the
Last days, the faithful disciples of
Jesus Christ who have lived in scorn
for the world and for themselves, in
poverty and in humility, in scorn and
in silence, in prayer and in mortification,
in chastity and in union with God, in
suffering and unknown to the world.*

It is time they come out and fill the
world with light. Go and reveal yourselves
to be my cherished children. I am at I
your side and within you, provided that
your faith is the light which shines
upon you in these unhappy days. May your
zeal make you famished for the glory and
the honor of Jesus Christ.

Fight, children of Light, you, the few
who can see. For now is the time of all
times, the end of all ends.

There will come a time when churches will close all over the globe. It is part of the New World Order. For those of us who miss the Rapture, we will be in a battle like we have never known.

Many Christians will be killed. The camps are in place around the world, lying in wait. For those who are fortunate and elude the enemy, escaping torture and certain death, a new life of exile will begin. Much like the early Christians who sought refuge in the Catacombs, Twenty-first Century Christians will have to survive underground. When John Paul II leaves Rome, it will signal to the Church that the time has come to go into hiding.

As the world slips into chaos and confusion, people will become more polarized. Under the Antichrist's leadership, Christians will be sought out.

Anne Catherine Emmerich said this in the early 1800's:

I saw more martyrs, not now but in

the future ... I saw the secret sect
relentlessly undermining the great
Church. Near them I saw a horrible beast
coming up from the sea. All over the
world, good and devout people, especially
the clergy, were harassed, oppressed, and
put into prison ...

Whole Catholic communities were being
oppressed, harassed, confined, and deprived
of their freedom. I saw many churches
closed down, great miseries everywhere,
wars and bloodshed. A wild and ignorant mob
took violent action. But it did not last
long...

According to prophecy, John Paul II will be found in exile, hunted down and killed. Before he dies, he will appoint his successor. His true successor will not be Gloria Olivae, but rather Petrus Romanus, the last pope in history.

Anne Catherine Emmerich spoke of this last pope as well as other visionaries, including Nostradamus, who described the last pope as "the great Roman." This last pope will have to steer the remnant church through the apocalypse. The last pope will go up against the Antichrist with his tattered remnant flock.

Some prophecies indicate that the last pope will be martyred, but there are also prophecies, which leave his death and its nature open, almost as if the end were not set in stone.

Petrus Romanus has been physically described as a small man who looks like he is of Jewish descent. Indeed, the man prophets have named as the last pope (over 500 throughout the world) is quite short in stature, around fifty years old and he is somewhat Jewish in appearance. Actually, the man is of Italian and German heritage.

Whether or not the visionaries are correct, whoever the last man is to sit in the chair of St. Peter will certainly have a great deal of work ahead of him.

Nostradamus indicates that Rome is headed for what might be described as a terrorist attack, perhaps a nuclear blow, which will signal the beginning of the Great Chastisement.

Abbess Maria Steiner, who was a visionary in the 1800's, had described the start of the chastisement.

I see the Lord as he will be scourging the world, and chastising it in a fearful manner so that few men and women remain. The monks will have to leave their monasteries, and the nuns will be driven from their convents, especially in Italy... The Holy Church will be persecuted...

Unless people obtain pardon through their prayers, the time will come when they will see the sword and death, and Rome will be without a shepherd.

Christians everywhere, not just Catholics, will suffer greatly in these times. It will be a wonder or miracle if any survive the perils of the Antichrist.

The Blessed Mother told Veronica Lueken this on May 14, 1977:

*The Holy Roman Catholic Church of
my Son will stand. The members shall
be reduced to few. Only a remnant, My
child, shall carry the banner Faithful
and True. But the gates of hell shall
fight a heavy battle against My Son's
Church, but they shall not succeed.*

So, how can a beleaguered remnant even hope to
win against incredible forces like those of the Antichrist? It
won't be because the remnant will have access to super
weapons, except perhaps prayer and the grace of God.

As mentioned in an earlier chapter, ground zero at
Nagasaki was survived by a group of holy priests. Still, it
would seem logical that these end-time few will need some
remarkable characteristics just to live in despicable times
let alone do battle against a formidable foe.

Another consideration is the communication
problem that will exist when society starts to crumble. In
order for the remnant to have any cohesiveness, certainly
communications will have to be available in some form.

Some prophets have mentioned that many end-time
people will have extraordinary capabilities. Apparently,
many saints in previous times had wanted to live in the
coming days because of the staggering graces God would
give to his people. The remnant will need all the blessings
God will allow just to have a glimmer of success.

Naturally, though, God in His wisdom will provide.
Mother Angelica of EWTN, has spoken about the end-
times where God's elect will be able to bi-locate, that is to
have the ability to be in more than one place at the same
time. Padre Pio had this ability, as did other saints. Bi-
location would definitely help relay communications from
group to group.

People will also be given the ability to heal the sick. This is of significant importance when medicines will not be able to kill the agonizing plagues. Certainly, healers will also win souls for God. Grateful people will have no doubt that God will be behind the cures.

The remnant will also have structure to it beyond Petrus Romanus. This structure will include twelve men chosen by Heaven who will be the end-times apostles. In the infancy of the Church there were the original twelve apostles. Now in the end-times, there will also be apostles and their disciples who will travel the world to feed Christ's sheep.

These apostles are already in place and they are ready to begin their apocalyptic apostolate. Their disciples will be even more help in giving solace to the surviving Church.

God has not forgotten the Jews in the end-times scenario. Modern prophets, as well as the Bible, mention the return of two men: Enoch and Elias, two prophets of the Old Testament, who will return to earth to fulfill their ministry, which is the conversion of the Jews. These two men were raptured and have been in a "holding" area, awaiting the final days of the era.

> *By faith Enoch was translated, that he should not*
> *see death; and he was not found, because God had*
> *translated him: for before his translation*
> *he had testimony that he pleased God.* (Heb. 11:5)

> *Behold I will send you Elias the prophet,*
> *before the coming of the great and dreadful*
> *day of the Lord.* (Mal. 4:5)

As they were walking along and talking
together, suddenly a chariot of fire and
horses of fire appeared and separated the
two of them, and Elias went up to heaven in
a whirlwind. (2 Kings 2:11)

Some Protestant ministers differ in the choice of the two witnesses mentioned in the Bible. Most agree that Elias will return, but, instead of Enoch, Moses may be the other prophet. The reason for this is taken from Matthew Chapter 17: 2-3:

And he was transfigured before them.
And his face did shine as the sun: and
his garments became white as snow. And
behold there appeared to them Moses and
Elias talking with him.

Since Enoch was not in the Transfiguration vision given to the Apostles, some Protestants believe neither of the witnesses will be Enoch.

Catholic visionaries disagree. In private revelations given to them by Heaven, Enoch is mentioned along with Elias. The Bible does defend the premise that both were raptured, that they did not die.

No matter if it's Moses or Enoch that returns with Elias, both witnesses will be stoned to death in Jerusalem. Their bodies will lie in the open for three days. After three days, they will rise. Mass Jewish conversions will take place at this point. Jews will be drawn away from the Antichrist. The following quotes from the Book of the Apocalypse, Chapter 11:3-8 foretells what is to come.

And I will given unto my two witnesses,
and they shall prophesy a thousand two
hundred and sixty days, clothed in sackcloth.

And if any man hurt them, fire shall come
out of their mouths, and shall devour their enemies.
And if any man will hurt him,
in this manner must he be slain.

These have the power to shut heaven,
that it rain not in the days of their
prophecy: and they have power over
waters to turn them into blood, and to
strike the earth with all plagues as
often as they will.

And when they shall have finished
their testimony, the beast that ascendeth
out of the abyss, shall make war against
them, and shall overcome them, and kill
them.

And their bodies shall lie in the streets
of the great city, which is called spiritually, Sodom
and Egypt, where their Lord was also crucified.

Refuges have also been started by the leaders of the remnant Church. These communities are built around their faith in God. A much simpler life style is found in these communities. Currently, the members of these groups are preparing their community for the monstrous times ahead.

Food is stocked, along with water, clothes, and sacramentals, all out of obedience to God.

Visionaries have mentioned these refuges, stating that a majority of them will be protected throughout the Tribulation. One visionary claims that heaven will send angels to protect the communities from the Antichrist and his troops. Others have mentioned that although the other areas of the world will be dry and desolate, the places of holy people will still be able grow crops. Their livestock will also be safe. It sounds like a heavenly oasis amidst the famine, drought and unthinkable bloodshed. Another visionary feels these refuges will either be made invisible by Heaven or that an unseen barrier will keep the world out.

Of course, God can do anything, but what about making a community invisible? History has shown as recently as the Twentieth Century, that God has indeed done this for visionaries. Theresa Neumann, a German seer and stigmatist lived in Hitler's Germany. One day, soldiers were sent to pick her up. Supposedly, Jesus appeared to Theresa and told her to stand in the corner while the soldiers ransacked the house looking for her. The SS troops searched the whole house, even glancing at the corner where she was standing, but they were not able to find her.

Another incident happened a few years ago in Rwanda. A woman who had been a visionary for some time was in church praying, along with most of her village. Troops came in and slaughtered everyone except the visionary, who was told to stand still by Heaven. The troops looked right through her but never saw her.

So, there is a precedent that Heaven has used invisibility as a defense for God's people. This defense is paramount in order for the fulfillment and culmination of prophecy.

St. John Bosco was an Italian priest who devoted his entire life to teaching boys to grow up to be good Christian men. He was also a mystic who had many prophetic dreams about our generation. One such dream follows.

*The vast expanse of water is covered
with a formidable array of ships in
battle formation, prows fitted with sharp,
spear-like beaks capable of breaking
through any defense.*

*All are heavily armed with cannons,
incendiary bombs, and firearms of all
sorts... and are heading towards one
stately ship, mightier than them all.
As they close in, they try to ram it,
set it afire, and cripple it as much
as possible.*

*This stately vessel is shielded by a
flotilla escort. Winds and waves are
with the enemy. In the midst of this
endless sea, two solid columns, a short
distance apart, soar high into the sky:
one is surmounted by a statue of the
Immaculate Virgin at whose feet a large
inscription reads: Help of Christians;
the other, far loftier and sturdier,
supports a Host of proportionate size
and beneath it bears the inscription:
Salvation of believers.*

Standing at the helm, the Pope strains
every muscle to steer his ship between
the two columns from whose summits hang
many anchors and strong hooks linked to
chains.

The entire enemy fleet closes in to
intercept and sink the flagship at all
costs. They bombard it with everything
they have: ...incendiary bombs, firearms,
cannons. At times a formidable ram
splinters a gaping hole into the hull,
but, immediately, a breeze from the
two columns instantly seals the gash.

Suddenly the Pope falls, seriously
wounded. He is instantly helped up but,
struck down a second time, dies. A shout
of victory rises from the enemy and wild
rejoicing sweeps their ships. But no
sooner is the Pope dead than another
takes his place. The captains of the
auxiliary ships elected him so quickly
that the news of the Pope's death coincides
with that of his successor's election. The
enemy's self-assurance wanes.

Breaking through all resistance, the
new Pope steers his ship safely between
the two columns and moors it to the two
columns; first, to the one surmounted
by the Host, and then to the other,
topped by the statue of the Virgin. At

this point, something unexpected happens.
The enemy ships panic and disperse,
colliding with and scuttling each other.

This dream relates the travails of what John Paul II will go through until his death. The dream also signifies Petrus Romanus taking the "helm" in his place. Victory is the final outcome of the dream, but not until Rome is sacked and the world plunged into war.

Our Lady at Fatima in 1917 foretold of this victory:

In the end, My Immaculate Heart will triumph.

Whether or not we are all unwitting players in these last days, it is evident that events are moving to the point where it will all collide. At this particular apex, we will find the Great Chastisement - like it or not, ready or not.

Chapter Fourteen

The Chastisement

There is no doubt that God loves us. We hear it in Church every Sunday, but there is something we do not hear that perhaps we should: God is just. We tend to forget that. Maybe that is the whole idea in this age of self-absorption. After all, even Church doctrines are changing, at least in America, where being politically correct is more important than being biblically correct. Even so, we are about to see the perfect justice of God.

Prophecies have indicated that America is due for a most horrific judgment because of abortion, lust and homosexuality. Some prophets have heard Heaven describe New York City as Babylon. Below is a sampling of these messages given to Veronica Lueken by Our Lady.

> *Your city is a cesspool! All the*
> *evils come as a nucleus here and fan*
> *out. When the hand comes upon you,*
> *you will be leveled for your licentiousness,*
> *your greed, your immorality...We cannot*

*turn the hourglass over, We cannot
start over, but We can lessen the
destruction that will come upon you.
Your city will be heavily struck by
the hand of the destroyer.*
                    (September 7, 1971)

*Babylon the great will fall. Babylon,
the master of deceit, will fall. Many
good must suffer as martyrs with the bad.
Babylon the great will fall! She has raised
herself high above her God, and she
invokes the vengeance of a just
punishment. Ships will look upon her as
she burns. Woefully, they will shield
their eyes from the sight.*

*Babylon, the great, the harlot upon
nations will fall. Babylon the great,
who has led many astray, will fall.*
                    (July 15, 1973)

*Your city We place as Babylon, your
city, the city of murder and evil,
corruption and godlessness, your city
will fall!*
                    (July 25, 1973)

*In your country there are areas, My
children, that will fall into major
catastrophe...*

The Bible has this to say about Babylon in The
Book of the Apocalypse, Chapter 18:2-3 and 18:8-11:

*And he cried out with a strong voice,
saying, Babylon the great is fallen,
is fallen: and is become the habitation
of devils, and the hold of every unclean
spirit, and the hold of every unclean
and hateful bird:*

*Because all nations have drunk of
the wine of the wrath of her fornication:
and the kings of the earth have committed
fornication with her: and the merchants
of the earth have been made rich by the
power of her delicacies.*

*Therefore shall her plagues come in
one day, death, and mourning and famine,
and she shall be burnt with the fire;
because God is strong, who shall judge her.*

*And the kings of the earth, who have
committed fornication, and lived in
delicacies with her, shall weep, and
bewail themselves over her, when they
shall see the smoke of her burning:
Standing afar off for fear of her torments,
saying: Alas! Alas!*

*That great city Babylon, that mighty city:
for in one hour is thy judgment come. And
the merchants of the earth shall weep
and mourn for her: for no man shall buy*

their merchandise any more.

New York City will not be the only city to be wiped out. Cities across this country will be destroyed within minutes. The whole of California will be decimated. As for the rest of the country, we are set for earthquakes, plagues, fires and civil unrest beyond our comprehension.

In another message to Veronica Lueken, Our Lady had this to say:

> *I repeat again, the earthquakes will*
> *increase in volume. California shall*
> *be struck. New York shall be struck.*
> *As I told you once before, there will*
> *be earthquakes in places that have never*
> *known a quake.*
>
> *It will startle them and frighten them*
> *but will they come to their knees? Few*
> *will, My child, because I can tell you*
> *this: They will not have the time to*
> *make amends; that is the sad part,*
> *My child...*

Floods will hit and then hit again. Previously, we have had a respite from natural disasters, but no more. We will be continually bombarded, one disaster after another, plague upon plague.

The rest of the world will not be immune. Another American visionary says that Heaven has specifically mentioned England is targeted for certain destruction if she does not change her ways. If she fails to change, the country will look like oyster crackers in the broth of the Atlantic Ocean. Only snippets of land will remain.

Australia and Japan are slated as well for a last dance with destiny. People will long for death, pulling their hair out with many people going insane. But the Bible says death will not come, not yet.

We should keep in mind all of the pestilence, plagues and natural disasters will be happening simultaneously along with the rise of the Antichrist. There is nothing that has gone before us to prepare us for the magnitude and the velocity of the Great Chastisement. Time is moving much faster dumping us into a vortex from which there is no escape. How can we know that the Chastisement is due?

> *Know also this, that in the last days,*
> *shall come dangerous times: Men shall be*
> *lovers of themselves, covetous, haughty,*
> *proud, blasphemers, disobedient to parents,*
> *ungrateful, wicked, without affection,*
> *without peace, slanderers, incontinent,*
> *unmerciful, without kindness, having an*
> *appearance indeed of piety, but denying*
> *the power thereof.* (2 Tim. 3:1-4)

Christina Gallagher, the Irish seer, had this vision of what approaches us:

> *I've seen Jesus, at another time,*
> *in the sky when He again expressed*
> *this firmness in His justice. This time,*
> *He lashed out at the sky with a scourge.*
> *When He did, I saw the sky burst into*
> *millions of cracks of lightning. Jesus*

was obviously very hurt by the sin of
the world; then, everything turned into
darkness. He repeated three times,
He wanted peace.

During this experience, beside Jesus,
on His right-hand side, was an angel
whom I recognized as the 'Angel of Wrath'
in red. The Angel of Wrath held in his
hand a cross of light with a circle around
this entire cross. From behind came a
white dove which perched on this cross
of light. I could hear thunder as the
lightning was cracking all over the sky.

I was neither up where Jesus was nor
was I on the earth. I was somewhere
in between. I was very, very
frightened. When the thunderbolts came,
it sounded as if the earth was exploding.
I looked down and I could see the road
open up, as if the buildings themselves
became sand and the people were falling
into the cracks. You could see the horror
and hear the screams. It was a really
horrible scene.

Then, I could see Our Blessed Mother
before Jesus and she looked very small.
I could only see Our Lady's mantle in
the shape of her, as if I was looking at
a back view of Our Blessed Mother. Our
Lady was crying and through the sobs of
tears, was saying, 'Mercy, my Son —

Mercy, my Son.

In a much more serious message, Christina was given this vision:

Tell all humanity to pray for the
Spirit of Truth, the Spirit of Love.
They are the one Spirit of Life Eternal.
Many pray, but live in the world and by
the world. They adore all of its fruits.
Oh, but the day is coming faster than
light, when My mighty Hand will crush
all in the world.

My daughter, you are little in the world.
You are rejected by the world. Know that
through this, you appease My anger. You
see with the eyes of the Spirit of Truth
and Love. That is why you suffer. Through
it, you appease My Wrath.

Today, offer Me My Divine Son,
through His wounds and Sacrifice,
that the world will prepare and make
itself ready for the Second Coming of
Jesus. As it is now, they prepare for
the forthcoming of the Antichrist.

Those who now live in the fruits of
the world and worship thus, will receive
of its fruits. They will drink of its
bitter cup, and become followers of

him-who-destroys.

*Tell all to prepare themselves. Make a
place in their hearts only for Me, their
Lord God, who desires to save. The battle
is on. Many souls are being lost. Go in
peace. Father, Son and Holy Spirit.*

Consider the twenty-one judgments listed in the
Bible that make up this appalling time.

THE SEAL JUDGMENTS

1. The rise of the Antichrist.
   (Rev. 6:1-2)

2. The largest and bloodiest war in history.
   (Rev. 6:3-4)

3. Global famine
   (Rev. 6:5-6)

4. The Pale Horse of Death spreads
   plagues.
   (Rev. 6:7-8)

5. God's people will be persecuted.
   (Rev. 6:9-10)

6. The earth will be an ecological disaster.
   Rev. 6:11-12)

7. Absolute terror.
   (Rev. 8:1)

THE TRUMPET JUDGMENTS

8.   The earth on fire.
     (Rev. 8:7)

9.   Oceans in tumult.
     (Rev. 8:8,9)

10. Water contamination.
     (Rev. 8:10,11)

11. Terrifying darkness.
     (Rev. 8:12)

12. All encompassing pestilence.
    (Rev. 9:1-6)

13. The world's greatest army.
    (Rev. 9:16)

14. A tremendous storm.
    (Rev. 11:15-19)

THE VIAL JUDGMENTS

15. Worldwide epidemic.
     (Rev. 16:2)

16 & 17. Oceans and rivers of blood.
(Rev. 16:3-7)

18. Incineration of the earth.
(Rev. 16:8,9)

19. Catastrophic plague.
(Rev. 16:10,11)

20. The largest invasion.
(Rev. 16:12)

21. The earthquake of all time.
(Rev. 16:18)

Another pertinent quote from the Bible that is relevant to this time comes in The Book of Apocalypse, Chapter 14:20:

And the press was trodden without
the city, and the blood came out of
the press, up to the horses' bridles,
for a thousand and six hundred furlongs.

Dr. Jack Van Impe has calculated this river of blood in today's units of measurement. It would be two hundred miles long, the entire length of Israel.

Eventually, the insanity will be global. The Antichrist will poise what is left of humanity on the brink of nuclear abrogation. Russia will move her troops towards Israel. In fact, all nations shall join in the fight against Israel.

In researching the likelihood of nuclear war, it was intriguing to find both the Old and New Testaments concur about the inevitability of nuclear war.

And by these three plagues was slain

a third part of men, by the fire and
by the smoke and by the brimstone, which
issued out of their mouths. (Rev. 9:18)

And I will show wonders in Heaven: and
in earth, blood and fire, and vapor of
smoke. (Joel 2:30)

For behold the day shall come kindled as
a furnace: and all the proud, and all that
do wickedly shall be stubble: and the day
that cometh shall set them on fire, saith
the Lord of Hosts, it shall not leave them
root, nor branch. (Mal. 4:1)

No matter whether we describe the Chastisement or Tribulation period as the punishment mentioned in Isiah, the trouble described in Jeremiah, or the wrath noted in Thessalonians, it all boils down to judgment.

The Protestant interpretation of the Tribulation is listed as eight sequential events.

1. The tribulation is ushered in with the rise of the Antichrist.

And I saw a beast coming up out of the sea, having
seven heads and ten horns, and upon his
horns ten diadems, and upon his heads names of
blasphemy. (Rev. 13:1)

2. Seven year Peace Contract between the Antichrist and Israel.

*And he shall confirm the covenant with
many, in one week...* (Dan. 9:27)

3. The Antichrist breaks the contract after forty-
two months.

*And in the half of the week the victim
and the sacrifice shall fail and there
shall be in the temple the abomination
of desolation: and the desolation shall
continue even to the consummation, and
to the end.* (Dan. 9:27)

4. The Russian Army moves south on Israel.

*And thou shalt come out of thy place from the
northern parts, thou and many people with thee,
all of them riding upon horses, a great company
and a mighty army.*

*And thou shalt come upon my people of Israel
like a cloud, to cover the earth. Thou shalt
be in the latter days, and I will bring thee
upon my land: that the nations may know me,
when I shall be sanctified in thee, O Gog,
before their eyes.* (Ez. 38:15-16)

5. God's people will be hunted by the
Antichrist. (Rev. 12.)

6. The Antichrist destroys the Church that brought
him to power.

And the ten horns which thou sawest in
the beast: these shall hate the harlot,
and shall make her desolate and naked,
and shall eat her flesh, and shall burn
her with fire. For God hath given into
their hearts to that which pleaseth him:
that they give their kingdom to the beast
till the words of God be fulfilled. (Rev. 17:16-17)

7.Proclamation by the Antichrist that he is God.

Who opposeth, and is lifted above all
that is called God, or that is worshipped,
so that he sitteth in the temple of God,
shewing himself as if he were God... (2 Thess. 2:4-11)

8.   The Antichrist is destroyed by God at Armageddon.

And I saw the beast and the kings of the
earth, and their armies gathered together
to make war with him that sat upon the
horse, and with his army. And the beast
was taken, and with him the false prophet,
who wrought signs before him, wherewith he
seduced them who received the character of
the beast, and who adored his image. These
two were cast alive into the pool of fire,
burning with brimstone. (Rev. 19:19-20)

The Catholic Church has the same chronology but some prophets have said that Heaven has informed them of a shortening to the Tribulation. It has also been suggested that time not only feels sped up, but actually has sped up because of the abbreviation of the Tribulation. The reason for the shortening is the fact that Jesus might not find anyone of faith left when he returns.

In the Book of Daniel, Chapter 12: 9-12, the prophet tells us when the daily sacrifice in the temple ceases (which the Antichrist will abolish) and the abomination is set up, there will be 1290 days or 3-and-a-half years.

> *And he said: Go Daniel, because the words are shut up, and sealed until the appointed time. Many shall be chosen, and made white, and shall be tried as fire:*
>
> *And the wicked shall deal wickedly, and none of the wicked shall understand, but the learned shall understand. And from the time when the continual sacrifice shall be taken away, and the abomination unto desolation shall be set up, there shall be a thousand two hundred and ninety days. Blessed is he that waiteth, and cometh unto a thousand three hundred and thirty five days.*

Our Lady reportedly told an Australian prophet about the time being shortened in the following messages. A table of calculations from this seer is included which may make it clearer.

*Your inspiration through the Holy Angels was
correct – time has speeded up by three hours
per month.* (July 28, 1994)

*My sweet child of the Holy Angels: what
you have been told is correct – that time
has again speeded up to seven hours a month
now. As the time of the Great Warning is near,
so will the time speed up, until there is
no more time."* (January 24, 1995)

*Time will be speeded up [after the Great
Warning] so that that fifteen minutes
duration will be one hour."*

*(Author's Note: If fifteen minutes equals one
hour, then the Antichrist's reign of three and
a half years will be completed in three hundred
and twenty days as shown below.)*

TIME SPEEDED UP

July 28, 1994
3 hours x 12
3 hours per month = 36 hours per year
2160 minutes per year
6 minutes per day

January 24, 1995
7 hours x 12
7 hours per month =   84 hours per year
                      5040 minutes per year
                      14 minutes per day

April 19, 1995
12 hours x 12
12 hours per month = 144 hours per year
                     8640 minutes per year
                     24 minutes per day

So when Our Lady says that all things can happen within one year of the Warning - The Miracle and the Great Chastisement, and Jesus' return - it is possible. I doubt if many people will be able to fathom all that will transpire. Visionaries recommend constant prayers to endure the times.

From the end-time prophecies relating to the Chastisement, it looks as though we will need all the prayers we can say. Scientists seem to be in agreement with this.

Jim Scotti, an astronomer, discovered an asteroid called 1997 XF-11. This asteroid made headlines when scientists calculated that this asteroid was heading straight for earth. The impact date was set for October 26, 2028. Shortly after the scientists involved made this declaration, NASA scrambled to refute it. They came up with new calculations and claimed that 1997 XF-11 would miss us by six hundred thousand miles.

Although there was relief, the doomsday news did cause people to think about what we as a planet would be facing in the event of a direct hit. The outlook is not good, which is what the prophets have been saying about the end time comet scenarios.

In messages given to Veronica Lueken, comets are mentioned several times.

> ...*Many will die, yes, this earth will*
> *be cleansed with a baptism of fire! Many*
> *will die in the great flame of the Ball of*
> *Redemption.*

> *When the Ball of Redemption comes upon*
> *your earth all will have received the*
> *Message from Heaven and they will have*
> *been given individual choice for their*
> *redemption.*

> *Those who have given their lives and*
> *souls to Lucifer are now blinded to what*
> *lies ahead. They will be eating and*
> *drinking and marrying, and then comes*
> *the Ball. Their flesh shall burn and*
> *dry up and blow off their bones as though*
> *it never existed. All those who have*
> *defamed their bodies, the temples of*
> *the Holy Spirit within them, these bodies*
> *will burn.*

> *...Scientists will look with fright*
> *as will the ordinary man. Know, My child,*
> *that no scientist will know an explanation*
> *for its appearance, the Ball of Redemption*
> *nears and many will die in the great flame*

of this Ball of Redemption.

Scientists have been keeping an eye on an asteroid called Toutatis. This particular "ball" has some eccentricities, which astronomers have been scrutinizing very carefully. French astronomers discovered Toutatis in 1989. It has an anomalous orbit, which is a four-year orbit that extends just inside Earth's orbit to the main asteroid belt between Mars and Jupiter. Toutatis' orbit is close to the plane of Earth's orbit than any known Earth-orbit-crossing asteroid.

Images of this asteroid indicate two irregular shaped objects that could be touching one another. One is approximately 2.5 miles wide and the other approximately 1.6 miles wide. This asteroid is particularly strange not only because of its unusual shape but also because of its "oddball" tumbling rotation. A side effect of the asteroid tumbling is that Toutatis doesn't have a fixed North Pole like Earth. "Stars viewed from Toutatis wouldn't repeatedly follow circular paths, but would criss-cross the sky, never following the same path twice," said Dr. Scott Hudson of Washington State University.

As one of the most chaotic asteroids out there, Toutatis has gained more watchers. Of particular end time interest is the fact that Toutatis will pass by Earth on September 29, 2004. It will be the closest pass of any known comet or asteroid between now and 2060.

Whether this "ball" or one like it will be part of the Warning or the Great Chastisement is difficult to say. However, this asteroid and its timing will be something to watch.

Other anomalies will take place with the Chastisement. Sadie Jaramillo relates this vision she had August 18, 1994:

I am preparing to receive communion,
with my eyes closed, when all of a sudden,
I see this flaming object with a tail of
flames, hurling through space downwards,
in total blackness.

I then see the same thing a second time,
only this time I can see a planet, way
off in the distance, such as when they
show shots from the moon of earth,
depicting it very small, very far away.
I see this object a third time, only
this time the object and the point of
impact (the planet) are as is only
seconds away.

I was overcome with sorrow and began to
cry and I kept saying Lord, what are you
trying to show me? Along with, No, no Lord,
I don't want to see anymore. Please don't
show me anymore. I don't want to know
anything else. I was overcome,
then after communion, during meditation,
I began to hear the voice of Our Lord and
He said:

I am Jesus, whom you have received and
made for Me a home of your heart. I have
just shown you what will cause man to
fall on his knees and know the dread
of his soul.

In 1976, Veronica Lueken was told of incredible loss of life because of the Ball of Redemption and other celestial bodies.

> *Now you are bargaining with the*
> *final count, My children. For as night*
> *will turn into day, and day will fall*
> *into darkness, that day will come when*
> *you will cry out for mercy, and it will*
> *be too late. The Ball of Redemption*
> *shall take from your earth three-quarters*
> *of mankind.*

> *Your country, America the beautiful,*
> *has not witnessed a massive scale of*
> *destruction and death. Is this what you*
> *call down upon yourselves? You, My children,*
> *hold the balance.*

Five years before this message was given, an eerie event took place at the Bayside Shrine where Veronica Lueken received her visions and messages. A man was visiting St. Robert Bellarmine Church in Queens, New York. Having his Polaroid camera with him, he decided to take a picture of the statue of Our Lady.

When the picture developed, the man noticed that something special had happened to his photo. Over the course of many years, several more miraculous photographs have been taken. This photograph in 1971 was indeed miraculous, especially because it was a huge piece of the end-time puzzle.

In the picture, you can the see statue of Our Lady, but in the foreground are the words: *Jacinta 1972*. This can be found in the picture section of this book.

The Blessed Mother later explained to Veronica just what this picture meant.

My child, the picture "Jacinta" must
be read by all of Earth's children. You
will give them this direction, My Child.
If it is in the will of the Eternal Father
that they be graced to receive the truth,
they will observe carefully and examine
the photograph miraculous "Jacinta 1972."
You will read the wording "Jacinta" and
search the lines and figures and numbers.
Within the miraculous picture is given the
date by God the Father for the Chastisement
of Mankind.

All will be conditional on the response
of mankind. You must well remember the
words of My Son to the World in relation
to this Miraculous Picture. Consider this
picture as a puzzle for the human race to
figure out.

The date for the Chastisement obviously was not meant to be 1972. As to the significance of 1972, that relates to a deathbed conversation Jacinta Marto had with a nun, Sister Godinho, who was caring for the dying child. Apparently, one of the secrets that Jacinta had heard at Fatima prompted her to tell the nun.

Jacinta asked Sister Godinho to pray that her order would forever remain loyal to the Vatican and that they needed to prepare themselves for the year 1972, "because man's sins would bring on the world such punishments and cause much suffering to the Holy Father."

Note the right side of the picture where the second "A" in Jacinta and the "2" create what looks like a bishop or pope's miter (hat).

Supposedly, Jacinta through her miraculous signature is indicating that the Antichrist was controlling many of the bishops and the pope was in danger. You will recall that Pope Paul VI was held hostage.

> *In the city of Rome there will be*
> *great confusion and trial. Satan,*
> *Lucifer in human form, entered into*
> *Rome in the year 1972. He (then) cut*
> *off the rule, the role, of the Holy*
> *Father, Pope Paul VI. Lucifer has*
> *controlled Rome (since that year), and*
> *he continues this control now.*

If you turn the picture clockwise, you can see the miter. Now turn the picture upright again. Remove the "J" and look at what remains.

A-C-I-N-T-O. Antichrist into the miter in 1972. The final infiltration of the Church by demonic forces would take place.

The Blessed Mother encouraged the proliferation of this photograph worldwide because the date, the hour and the time of the Great Chastisement are hidden in the words, numbers and lines. The picture may be turned sideways or upside down in order to extract the information. Not everyone will be given the grace to see dates. What do you see?

Another interpretation of this picture is that the *1972* mentioned within pertains to the anniversary of Christ's crucifixion. The year 2005 would mark the 1972nd anniversary of Christ's death.

The Second Coming of Jesus will occur shortly after the Great Chastisement. However, there are still two more horrors to endure: the final nuclear war and the Three Days of Darkness.

Chapter 15

The Three Days Of Darkness

One of the realities my research has uncovered time and time again is that scripture must be fulfilled. No matter who the visionary is, or what the message is, one of the main threads among all of them is the fact that these end-times must happen. All that has been prophesied will come true. The extent and depth of the actualization depends on how much we pray. Many of the predicted events have been postponed due to prayer. Other events have been lightened also because of prayer.

Yet, no matter what, we cannot stop the hand of God, the end of the era or our final destiny.

Most people cannot imagine that our planet will survive the cataclysm. Still we are reminded in a prayer that Catholics say everyday:

> *Glory be to the Father, and to the*
> *Son, and to the Holy Spirit. As it was*
> *in the beginning, is now and ever*
> *shall be, WORLD WITHOUT END.*

After the fires burn out, after the nukes stop exploding, after the dust clears there will be the new era, the new springtime. To reach that new dawn, first we have to brave the final nuclear war and the Three Days of Darkness.

Allan Rudio, a gentle Filipino visionary was a boy when he started getting messages from Heaven. On April 6, 1994, Allan received a message from the Blessed Mother telling him that man must turn from sin or the following would happen:

1.   Earthquakes will last 24 hours.

2.   The sun will spin with a great explosion.

3.   Stars will fall from the sky.

4.   Fires from Heaven will fall.

5.   The Three Days of Total Darkness

Describing the days right before the Three Days of Darkness, Jesus said this to Allan on July 1, 1994:

> *...Pray, prepare for the three days*
> *of darkness is coming. No devils will*
> *be left in hell, all with be here...It is*
> *[3 days] darkness everywhere, you won't be*
> *able to see your own hands. But, on the*
> *fourth day all things will be new.*

Just preceding the Three Days of Darkness, all out nuclear war will erupt. The Antichrist, in a last effort to triumph, will initiate this battle. As the armies of the world bear down on Israel, the Antichrist and his agents will unleash all the nuclear arsenals in the world. One of the major reasons that the Antichrist will be compelled to launch the nuclear weapons are the miraculous and permanent images left behind after the Great Miracle.

With all his ruinous behavior and the slaughter of millions of souls, the Antichrist or Lucifer will feel he has won the right to return to Heaven. Visionaries whose messages cover the Three Days of Darkness agree that Lucifer will try to "ascend" into heaven but that God will swat him like a fly, knocking him down to hell.

There is also a consensus of opinion about the signs to look for that indicate the Three Days of Darkness are imminent:

1. The night will be terribly cold. The wind will roar and howl. Then the lightening will start, thunderbolts and earthquakes as well. The stars and planets will be disturbed. Their positions will be altered in the sky. There will be absolutely *no* light, just total blackness, complete darkness will engulf the earth. This will be immediate or come suddenly.

2. Not a single demon will be left in hell. Every evil spirit will be released, free to roam the earth. They will do all possible harm to souls. Demons will appear in frightening forms, filling the air with pestilence and poisonous gases. Terrifying apparitions will abound. Many will die from fear and despair. The wicked people will see the Divine Heart of God.

My angels, who are to be the executioners
of this work, stand ready with pointed swords
and they will take special care to annihilate
all those who have mocked Me and would believe
in my revelations.

3.   From Heaven hurricanes of fire will be cast onto the earth. Fear will consume mortals at the sight of the clouds of fire. God's wrath will be poured out on the entire world.

4.   Before Satan is cast into Hell by God, he will appear to triumph. It will appear as though Hell has captured the world. But God will reclaim it.

What can we do to protect ourselves? We have been told by seers and mystics that, as soon as we see the disturbing signs, to go immediately inside, shut and lock all doors and windows. Do not go out for any reason. As in the Warning, the wrath of God is holy and we are not permitted to see it.

The only thing that will burn are blessed beeswax candles (51 – 100%). Light them right away. However, these candles, even if blessed, will not burn in the homes of the godless or the scoffers. Once the candles are lit, nothing will put them out. Keep plenty of candles on hand along with Holy Water to be sprinkled around the house, especially the doors and the windows. Bless yourself and others with it. Drink it and anoint your eyes, ears, nose, throat, feet, hands and forehead.

As recommended in earlier chapters, keep extra food and water stored. Kneel down in front of a crucifix and pray incessantly. Call on God's mercy, for it knows no bounds. Invoke the angels and saints to help you. God will purge the world during this time and no sinner on earth will be able to escape. Jesus told one visionary: "I will find them all."

Veronica Lueken was told on September 7, 1973 that:

> *Your future is now. The decision*
> *for man's extinction, his destruction,*
> *lies now with man. The Father watches;*
> *He waits as you approach great days of*
> *darkness.*

I mentioned in an above paragraph on God's Mercy. Sister Faustina, a Polish nun, who was recently canonized, had fourteen years of messages from Jesus on the subject of Divine Mercy and all that it meant.

> *I remind you daughter, that as often*
> *as you hear the clock strike the third*
> *hour (3:00 p.m.) immerse yourself*
> *completely in My mercy, adoring and*
> *glorifying it; invoke its omnipotence*
> *for the whole world, and particularly*
> *for poor sinners;*
>
> *For at that moment mercy was opened wide*
> *for every soul. In this hour you can*
> *obtain everything for yourself and for*
> *others for the asking; it was the hour*
> *of grace for the whole world – mercy*
> *triumphed over justice.*

Evidently, the Chaplet of Divine Mercy is very powerful. Sister Faustina had another message from Jesus for the critical hour that approaches us all:

> *At the hour of their death, I defend*
> *as My own glory every soul that will*
> *say this chaplet; or when others say*
> *it for a dying person, the indulgence*
> *is the same.*

> *When this chaplet is said by the bedside*
> *of a dying person, God's anger is*
> *placated, unfathomable mercy envelops*
> *the soul, and the very depths of My*
> *tender mercy are moved for the sake of*
> *the sorrowful Passion of My Son.*

The Divine Mercy Chaplet is listed in the back of the book along with other important prayers. These messages of Divine Mercy offer great hope and consolation. Whenever our personal "critical" time arrives, either in the Warning, the Great Calamities, the Plagues or the Great Chastisement, we always have God. It is with God that over one billion people will survive the Great Chastisement and enter into the Reign of Peace, but not until Jesus returns.

Chapter 16

The Second Coming

Many of the end-time events will be happening simultaneously. The Chastisements will hit as the world troops surround Jerusalem followed by the Three Days of Darkness. Things will progress in rapid succession. It is at this time that Christ will descend from Heaven to the Mount of Olives.

From the Protestant perspective, several points are met right before Jesus returns.

- Advent of automobiles. (Na. 2:3-4)

- Conception of the airplane. (Isa. 31:5)

- Flowers and plants start to grow and bloom in the desert. (Isa. 35:1)

- The ten-nation alliance. (Dan. 2:7).

- Knowledge explosion. (Dan. 12:4)

- Worldwide travel is commonplace. (Dan. 12:4)

- Many false Christs. (Matt. 24:5,24; 2 Peter 2:1)

- War is prevalent. (Mark 13:7)

- The gospel preached in all the world (Matt. 24:14)

- Celestial signs and changes. (Luke 17:26-30, 21:25-27)

- Evil spirits dominate. (1 Tim. 4:1,2)

- The signs of 2 Timothy 3:1-5

- Gold and silver hoarded and then their loss of value. (James 5:1-3)

- False prophets deny the divinity of Christ. (2 Pet. 2:1-3)

- Increased scoffers regarding the Second Coming. (2 Pet. 3:3,4)

- Nuclear weapons invented. (2 Peter 3:10)

- The judgments found in the Book of Revelation 6-18

- God's people are lukewarm. Compared to Revelation 3:14-16

All of these things are at least in motion if not basically fulfilled.

In September of 1985, Veronica Lueken was told this by Jesus:

> *Do not follow the scoffers who continue*
> *to say, "His promise has not and will not*
> *come true, to return in the Second Coming."*
> *I assure you I shall come to you all as*
> *a thief in the night.*
>
> *Little will you be prepared unless you*
> *listen to My Mother's counsel and keep*
> *your heart open for the truth. the more*
> *you seek riches in this life, the less*
> *you will have in Heaven, for they do not*
> *coincide. My child and My children. You*
> *cannot have a god, symbolized by money,*
> *before you, for you will love one and hate*
> *the other. And whom will you hate,*
> *My children, but Me?*

St. Thomas Aquinas mentions in the Summa Theologica that St. Jerome attributed fifteen signs that would immediately precede the judgment.

- On the first day all the seas will rise fifteen cubits above the mountains;

- In the second day all the waters will be plunged into the depths, so that scarcely will they be visible;

- On the third day they will be restored to their previous condition;

- On the fourth day all the great fishes and other things that move in the waters will gather together and, raising their heads above the sea, roar at one another contentiously;

- On the fifth day, all the birds of the air will gather together in the fields, wailing to one another, with neither bite nor sup;

- On the sixth day rivers of fire will arise towards the firmament rushing together from the west to the east;

- On the seventh day all the stars, both planets and fixed stars, will throw out fiery tails like comets;

- On the eighth day there will be a great earthquake, and all animals will be laid low;

- On the ninth day all the plants will be bedewed as it were with blood;

- On the tenth day all stones, little
  and great, will be divided into four
  parts dashing against one another;

- On the eleventh day all hills and
  mountains and buildings will be reduced
  to dust;

- On the twelfth day all animals will
  come from forest and mountain to the
  fields, roaring and tasting of nothing;

- On the thirteenth day all graves from
  east to west will open to allow the
  bodies to rise again;

- On the fourteenth day all men will
  leave their abode, neither understanding
  nor speaking, but rushing hither and
  thither like madmen;

- On the fifteenth day all will die and
  will rise again with those who died
  long before.

The signs mentioned by St. Jerome are not from him but, rather, he ascribes them to the Hebrews, having found them in their annals.

Whatever their origin, God in His goodness gives us signs to prepare ourselves for judgment. There are those who argue that the signs listed in the Protestant account have been here since the human race began. For instance, floods and earthquakes were prevalent, and certainly wars and rumors of wars have always accompanied us.

However, Billy Graham believes that the signs are now more prevalent and that all the signs are starting to converge.

St. Augustine thought that the end of the era would be near when the good will be persecuted by the wicked. In other words, the good will fear and the wicked will feel safe. 1 Thessalonians, 5:3, states, "For when they shall say, peace and security; then shall sudden destruction come upon them." This will refer to the wicked after the Antichrist is dead and they will pay no attention to the signs.

Biblical chronology describes approximately six thousand years from Adam and Eve to the year 2000 AD God has "leased" us the earth for six thousand years. After that time, scholars agree that mankind will be in transition. Early Christian writers thoroughly believed in the six thousand-year history of man.

Barnabas wrote:

As there has been 2000 years from
Adam to Abraham, and 2000 years from
Abraham to Christ; so there will be
2000 years for the Christian Era and
then would come the Millennium.

This new millennium will be the Reign of Peace with Jesus as King.

A father of the Church, St. Iranaeus said:

For the day of the Lord is a thousand
years; and in six days created things

were completed; it is evident therefore,
that they will come to an end at the six
thousand years.

St. Lacatantius, a man who tutored the son of
Constantine, wrote in his Book of Divine Interpretations in
Chapter Fourteen:

Let the philosophers know that the
six thousandth year is not yet completed;
and when this number is completed, the
consummation must take place.

Even Jewish writers are in agreement with the
timeframe for the Messiah to come. It is mentioned
frequently in the Talmud and refers to the six thousand-
year period. One Talmudic researcher, Tanna debe
Eliyyahu, has stated that he believes the world would exist
for six thousand years. He sees the first two thousand years
as desolation in that there was no Torah. This is the period
from Adam to Abraham.

Eliyyahu calls the next two thousand years a time
when the Torah flourished. The following two thousand
years were Messianic and the time in his opinion when the
Messiah should have come. Eliyyahu felt that it was
because of the Jews sins that Christ did not appear.

In actuality, many Jews did not realize that the first
coming of the Messiah would be secret. Christ would not
arrive as the King they were expecting, but he will return as
the King the Jews have sought for so long. The irony is that
Eliyyahu thought the Messiah did not come because of our

sins, but the reality is He did come *because* of the sins of man.

God is very dogmatic and places strong emphasis on the Sabbath, both literally and spiritually. Therefore since a thousand years to the Lord is a day, (Psalm 90:4; 2,) both ancient and modern scholars view the seventh millennium as the Sabbath Millennium. This Sabbath Millennium has prophetic overtones. God created the world in six days. On the seventh day, God rested. God's "work" with men will be at an end and Jesus will sit on the throne, His work completed.

The Bible is very clear that Christ would not return until Israel would be a nation in its own right. That has happened as mentioned earlier. Some biblical scholars feel that satanic power through the course of history was trying to prevent the rise of Israel. To the experts, Herod was used by Satan to kill all male children under the age of two in hopes that Jesus would be killed. Again, they felt Hitler was used by Satan to exterminate the Jewish population to prevent them from returning to Israel in order to build an Israeli nation. As testimony to God's truth that prophecy must be fulfilled, the Jewish State did come into existence in spite of the holocaust.

God always has meaning in what He says or does. His use of particular numbers - 3, 7, 40 and 70 - and their repetition shows patterns in God's work with mankind.

The three-day pattern of restoration can be found with Jonah and his deliverance from the great fish. Most importantly was Jesus' resurrection from the dead.

Looking now at the number seven, we can evaluate the seven-year cycle. A servant under Hebrew law was to serve his master for six years and would be set free in the seventh year without paying anything. (Ex. 21:2)

Therefore, if our debt were paid in the sixth millennium, God's return in the seventh millennium would set us free.

If you examine Jubilee years, we are approaching the seventieth Jubilee. When the Jews entered the Promised Land over thirty-five hundred years ago, God instructed the Jews to observe a "Year of Jubilee" every fifty years. In the year 2000, or shortly thereafter, we will mark the seventieth Jubilee. Interestingly, it would also make the fortieth Jubilee from when Jesus began His ministry. That in itself was the thirtieth year of Jubilee. At that time, Jesus was thirty years old.

Solomon's reign is considered symbolic of the Millennium. There is also symbolism to be found in the temple Solomon had been building. The Temple was 120 cubits high. One hundred and twenty priests blew trumpets (Chronicles 5:12). The Queen of Sheba gave Solomon 120 talents of gold. (Chronicles 9:9). It was mentioned that Jewish Jubilee years were marked by periods of fifty year duration. Genesis states that man's days will be limited to 120 years. Some physicians feel man's cell duplication capability exhausts itself after 120 years.

The 120 years found in Genesis may be expressed as 120 x 50 (Jubilee Years) which equals 6000 years of man's existence.

Outside of the Bible, angel sightings and their messages have grown significantly. The angels all have the same message that Jesus is coming "very, very soon."

Even if you do not believe in modern-day prophets, the Bible is quite clear that the Lord is coming and that our redemption draws nigh.

After Jesus returns and frees us, a new day will dawn following the Three Days of Darkness. On that glorious day we will step out into a wonderful new world. From the black and white starkness of the Chastisement, we will open our doors and see a colorful, lush new earth, transformed for us by God. Just as Dorothy regained consciousness, walked to her door in grainy shades of gray and then opened the door to a technicolor wonder, so we will then find ourselves over the rainbow. The Reign of Peace will be ours.

Chapter 17

The Reign Of Peace

It is apparent that the Reign of Peace, as seen by hundreds of visionaries, has a central theme. The following description of the Reign of Peace represents the consensus of those visionaries.

The Reign of Peace will literally be paradise on earth. Not since Adam and Eve were driven out of the garden of Eden has there been anything that compares to it. Imagine a world of crystal clean water, skies free from pollution and a temperature of 72 degrees each and every day. Gorgeous trees and lush grass will be everywhere. Crops will be abundant. Animals of all kinds will be plentiful and will get along with each other.

The Blessed Mother told Veronica Lueken about the reign in March of 1973:

> *My poor children, hopeless of heart,*
> *know now that the future after the*
> *cleansing will be glorious, far more*
> *glorious than your human mind could*
> *ever conceive. Beauty of beauties!*
> *Emotion superb! The pursuement of*
> *every desire that man could conceive*

on earth will be yours in the Kingdom.
Is this, My children, what you will
discard for the few short earthly years
given to you, as you run about aimlessly
seeking the pleasures of your world and
the riches, willing to close your hearts
and your ears to the truth?

Violence will be totally removed from society. No longer will there be a need for politicians, different governments or even for money. It will be quiet as well. We won't have cars or planes. Nothing that runs on electricity or fuel will make it into the Reign of Peace. If you think back in American history, the Reign will be very similar to the early 1800s. Horses will again be the source of transportation. For the most part, life in the Reign will be agricultural. The need for large cities will be nonexistent.

The seventh millennium will be a holy time. Jesus will be with us in the Reign, teaching us and guiding us towards perfection. Although this will be paradise, it will not be heaven. Those of us who make it to the Reign will still have to grow spiritually. However, it will be a time of no distractions or temptations. All evil will be relegated to Hell until the Final Judgment.

Twelve territories will exist in the Reign. Each of these territories will be called by the names of the original tribes of Israel. These territories will have queens, princes and kings, who will oversee the people. Moreover, these "monarchs" will be nothing like what we associate with when we think of rulers today. We will know these rulers by their titles and they will live in special places. They can be compared to governors but will not be more important that the consummate King, Jesus, and His mother, The Queen.

Each of those people who make it to the Reign are descendants of one of the twelve tribes of Israel. Upon entering into the Reign, all your family from around the globe will be united and live in towns or communities of that tribe.

The communities will have Churches and schools. Everyone in the community will pray daily, together and individually. This will be a time totally devoted to God.

There will be many blessings given to us by God. Many signs and wonders will astound us. One of the many joys we will be allowed is the return of our pets who may have died several years ago or during the Tribulation.

We will also be allowed, according to some visionaries, to stand at the gate of the New Jerusalem and see Purgatory, which is below us, or see Heaven above us. However, we will not be able to visit.

It will not be an easy time of transition for us to go from a modern world of conveniences to a more pioneer state. For this reason, it will take approximately forty years to assimilate the different living conditions and to adjust to the new world.

Some people will find out that the pioneer lifestyle is not for them. They may wish to die and go to Heaven, which God will allow. For others, life expectancy will be greatly increased to one hundred, two hundred, or several hundred years. All life has a timeline and God ordains the lifespan of each person. When death comes, it will not be painful since all who die in the Reign will go straight to Heaven. The Tribulation, Chastisement and the Reign account for any purgatorial suffering.

In the Reign, many, many children will be born. Some visionaries indicated this is because of the vast number of souls who have gone to hell over the past few hundred years, but especially in our time. Many mansions are empty in Heaven and God, therefore, wants them filled.

Childbirth will not be as we know it now. It will be painless. There will also be many multiple births. According to some visionaries, several billion children will be born.

As I mentioned, not everyone will make it into the Reign. First of all, you have to want to go there and then you must ask God to give you that grace. It has been recommended by several visionaries that we reform our lives now. By turning off the television, computers, and stereos and by spending more time in prayer, we can transform the way we live. God must be the focal point.

According to all of the visionaries who have been told of the Reign, we must be in a state of grace, free from mortal sin and try to reduce the venial sins we commit.

In the Reign, people will still sin, not major sins, but more through vices we bring into the Reign from the past. This spiritual baggage will be removed with time. Each successive generation will be further along the path of perfected spirituality and the love of God.

God gave to us the prophecy on the Reign very early in history with the intention of providing hope and the desire to participate in the Reign. The Reign is also a time to cleanse away original sin. This cleansing restores mankind to its original condition before Adam and Eve's downfall. It will also be a time when our hearts grow closer to God.

The Reign will last somewhere between one thousand and fifteen hundred years. One of the reasons for this will be the souls in purgatory. These souls may still have a great deal of time left to serve in Purgatory. Since they cannot pray for themselves, the people in the Reign must pray for them so that their suffering will be alleviated. Graces for the poor souls will increase greatly because of the sacrifices of people alive in the Reign.

Another reason was the building up of the Body of Christ, as stated earlier, which will be necessary to fill the houses in Heaven.

The third reason is the generational cleansing process, which will take at least one thousand years. We will also have, according to visionaries, extraordinary help during our perfection process. Saints in Heaven will be allowed to assist us and to instruct us on the best way to meet our spiritual goals. If this is true, think of the incredible conversations we could have with truly the best and the brightest. Even though the rustic lifestyle may be difficult, having the saints to help us would surely be tremendous.

When speaking with people about the Reign and the lifestyle that will be found there, so many have answered that they would miss things like coffee, cell phones and pizza deliveries. Just the thought of going without a hair dryer gives me pause. Perhaps the best way to describe the change would be extreme culture shock.

Wouldn't we all be happier without the fax machines, the pagers and phones bothering us all day? The slower pace has got to be refreshing and definitely a great deal healthier.

I think the reason people can't grasp living with Jesus in the Reign without our conveniences is that much of our modern lifestyle excludes God. We are too busy and have become slaves to our conveniences. So, in essence, the high-tech toys have become idols which separate us from the Creator. We think we have it all when in reality, we have nothing. In the Reign we will have God and a sense of happiness and fulfillment which we make impossible now. If the Reign is everything that the prophets say it is, I would bet we won't have much of a withdrawl from the gizmos and ulcerating schedules.

We will bathe in the pristine waters of the Jordan and be thoroughly cleansed without the antibacterial soap and strawberry shampoo. If you really like that strawberry fragrance you can make your own soap or barter for some.

There will be great fishing and hunting. The crops will grow to maturity every month. Sure, the learning process of mulling grain, tanning hides, spinning wool and making clothes will take time, but we will have help.

It has been recommended to visionaries that we get those how-to books now and teach ourselves how to be self sufficient. In some ways, and to many people, this may seem like hard work. That it is, but it will be the quintessential opportunity. There will be no more hunger, no more sickness and no more wars.

The visionary Allan Rudio was given three things that we need to do if we want to go to the Reign of Peace:

- *Ask Jesus to give you the courage that you may pass the coming of the tribulation.*

- *Consecrate yourselves to the Immaculate Heart of Mary three times a day.*

- *Do the seven keys to Heaven.*

Following the Reign of Peace, the Last Judgment will occur. The prophets of old referred to this as the "Day of the Lord." It is a time when all nations will be called to judgment.

Jesus spoke of this judgment in Matthew 25:31-33:

And when the Son of Man shall come
in his majesty, and all the angels
with him, then shall he sit upon the
seat of his majesty. And all nations
shall be gathered before him, and he
shall separate them one from another,
as the shepherd separateth the sheep
from the goats: And He shall set the
sheep on his right hand, but the goats
on his left.

The last judgment is considered an article of faith in all ancient creeds. In the Apostles Creed it is mentioned:

He ascended into Heaven. From thence
He shall come to judge the living and
the dead.

In the Nicene Creed it states:

He shall come again in glory to judge
the living and dead.

The Athanasian Creed affirmed the above:

From thence he shall come to judge
the living and dead, at whose coming
all men must rise with their bodies
and are to render an account of their deeds.

People have wondered for thousands of years why there would be a general judgment following an individual judgment. In the Roman Catechism, the reason is explained:

> *The first reason is founded on*
> *the circumstances that most augment*
> *the rewards or aggravate the punishments*
> *of the dead. Those who depart this life*
> *sometimes leave behind them children*
> *who imitate the conduct of their parents,*
> *descendants, followers; and others who*
> *adhere to and advocate the example, the*
> *language, the conduct of those on whom*
> *they defend, and whose example they*
> *follow; and as the good or bad influence*
> *or example, affecting as it does the conduct*
> *of many, is to terminate only with this*
> *world, justice demands that, in order to*
> *form a proper estimate of the good or bad*
> *actions of all, a general judgment should*
> *take place...*
>
> *Finally, it was important to prove, that*
> *in prosperity and adversity, which are*
> *sometimes the promiscuous lot of the good*
> *and of the bad, everything is ordered by*
> *an all wise, all-just, and all-ruling*
> *Providence; it was therefore necessary*
> *not only that rewards and punishments*
> *should await us in the next life, but*
> *that they should be awarded by a public*
> *and general judgment.*

Again, signs are given concerning the nearness of the General Judgment. These signs and predictions were not intended to give the exact date. The following list details what we should look for.

- Christianity preached throughout the world.

And the gospel of the kingdom
shall be preached in the whole world, for
a testimony to all nations and then shall
the consummation come." (Matt. 24:14)

- Final conversion of the Jews.

St. Paul to the Romans, 11:25-26, states,
For I would not have you ignorant,
brethren, of this mystery... that blindness
in part has happened in Israel, until the
fullness of the Gentiles should come in.

- Enoch and Elias return. Malachias 4:5-6 states:

Behold I will send you Elias the prophet,
before the coming of the great and
dreadful day of the Lord. And he shall
turn the heart of the fathers to the
children, and the heart of the children
to their fathers: lest I come, and strike
the earth with anathema.

Ecclesiasticus 44:16 also states:

*Enoch pleased God and was transplanted
into Paradise, that he may give repentance
to the nations.*

- The horrible apostasy. St. Paul warned the
  Thessalonians not to be afraid as if the Day of
  the Lord were near, for a revolt must occur first:

*Let no man deceive you by any means, for
unless there come a revolt first, and the man
of sin be revealed, the son of perdition,
who opposeth, and is lifted up above all
that is called God, or that is worshipped,
so that he sitteth in the temple of God,
showing himself as if he were God.*
(2 Thess. 2:3-4)

- The Antichrist comes to power.

*Little children, it is the last hour; and as
you have heard that Antichrist cometh,
even now there are become many
Antichrists: whereby we know that is
the last hour.* (1 John 2:18)

- Cataclysmic upheaval in nature. Matthew 24:29
  and Luke 21:25-26:

*And immediately after the tribulation of
those days, the sun shall be darkened and
the moon shall not give her light, and the
stars shall fall from Heaven, and the powers
of heaven shall be moved.*

*And there shall be signs in the sun,
and in the moon, and in the stars; and
upon the earth distress of nations, by
reason of the confusion of the roaring
of the sea and of the waves; Men withering
away for fear, and expectation of what
shall come upon the whole world. For the
powers of Heaven shall be moved.*

- A worldwide holocaust.

*But the day of the Lord shall come as
a thief, in which the heavens shall pass
away with great violence, and the elements
shall be melted with fear, and the earth
and the works which are in it, shall be
burnt up. Seeing then that all these
things are to be dissolved, what manner
of people ought you to be in holy
conversation and godliness? Looking
for and hasting unto the coming of the
day of the Lord, by which the heavens
being on fire shall be dissolved and
the elements shall melt with burning
heat? But we look for new heavens and
a new earth according to his promises,
in which justice dwelleth.* (2 Pet. 3:10-13)

- The last trumpet.

In a moment, in the twinkling of an

eye, at the last trumpet: for the
trumpets shall sound, and the dead
shall rise again incorruptible: and we
shall be changed. (Cor. 15:52)

For the Lord himself shall come down
from heaven with commandment, and with
the voice of an archangel, and with the
trumpet of God: and the dead who are
in Christ, shall rise first. (Thess. 4:16)

- Jesus returns.

And then shall appear the sign of the
Son of man in heaven: and then shall all
tribes of the earth mourn: and they shall
see the Son of man coming in the clouds
of heaven with much power and majesty.
(Matt. 4:16)

The Blessed Mother has told a few visionaries that the General Judgment would be Jesus' Third Advent. With this third advent, it is felt we will be judged in the air. Some scholars cite 1 Thessalonians 4:16 for this.

Then we who are alive, who are left,
shall be taken up together with them
in the clouds to meet Christ, into
the air, and so shall we be always
with the Lord.

According to Joel 3:2, the place of the last judgment is the Valley of Josaphat.

I will gather together all nations,
and will bring them down into the valley
of Josaphat: and I will plead with them
there for my people, and for my inheritance
Israel, whom they have scattered among the
nations, and have parted my land.

Both the good and the bad will be called to Judgment, all made to account for their deeds. It has also been debated as to whether or not the good and the bad angels will be judged at this time. However, the angels and demons have already established their eternal destiny. They will get a pronouncement of judgment at a later time to account for their good or bad council of men.

The object of the Judgment is to lay bare all works, positive and negative. Even sins that have been forgiven will be measured with the unforgiven sins. Every secret thought will be judged (1 Cor. 4:5). Most theologians teach that even the secret thoughts of the saints will be judged. This is believed to be accurate because it will make justice complete.

Commentators on sacred scripture refer to Matthew 25:31-46 and The Book of Apocalypse 20:12 for an account of the form Judgment will take. Each person's conduct will be made plain to each individual's conscience and to the general knowledge of those assembled. It is believed that no words will be spoken at the Judgment but rather we will all receive instantaneous Divine Illumination as mentioned in Romans 2:15:

Who shew the work of the law written
in their hearts, their conscience bearing

witness to them, and their thoughts between
themselves accusing, or also defending one another.

When Jesus says "Come, ye blessed or depart from me," that will conclude the judgment and seal the destiny of mankind. All will be explained and justified.

Conclusion

Wherever we place our faith, either in God or things of the world, it will be tested in the days to come. I am certain that there will be people who will arrive late to the party, people who hedge their bets one way or the other.

Yet, in the last analysis, we will all know if we have chosen correctly. Ultimately, some people's faith and the things in which they place their trust will crumble. If we put our trust in the tangible, the stuff we can see and feel, we might have something solid - something we can grasp at least.

On the other hand, if we put our faith and trust in the intangible, the things we can't see or feel, I believe we will be able to hold on forever. We will also be held by the loving hand of God, who will never loosen His grip.

To some, it may be easy to scoff at the messages presented in this book. They might be too real or too far out for us to pay any attention to them.

What, then, if they *are* real? If the prophets are correct, what will we do? Each of us has a decision to make. The main themes of these messages can be checked off one by one as they occur. Seconds will tick down until the watch finally stops.

No matter what our position is at this very moment, it will change. Perhaps one of the last questions we will ever have to answer will be, "Do you choose Eternal Life or the Death of the Damned?"

Pictures

Invasion map reportedly given to Andrew Wingate by Heaven. The arrows depict where the troops are expected to enter the United States and Canada (see page 21).

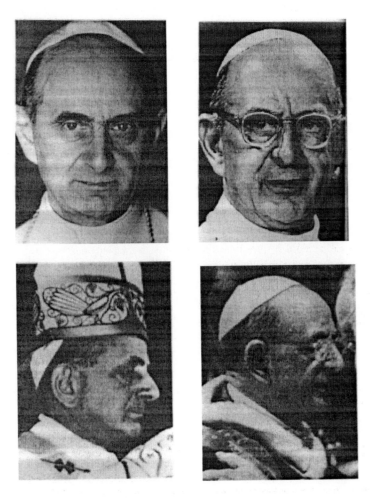

Pictures of both the real Pope Paul VI and the impostor
pope. Pope Paul VI is on the left-hand side of the page,
while the impostor is on the right. Note the sharp nose of
Pope Paul VI compared to the stubbier nose of the
impostor. Notice a difference in the upper lips, length of
their noses, and the difference in ear size and shape (see
page 42).

<u>2a</u> pe cca t o r u m ve st r o r u m
Voice of "the Pope" on Easter, 1975
("the Pope" is Pope Paul VI)

<u>2b</u> pe cca t o r u m ve st r o r u m
Voice of "the Pope" on Christmas, 1975
("the Pope" is the Impostor)

Another picture of the impostor pope, as well as the voiceprints of the two men (see page 44).

The four Garabandal visionaries: from the left, Conchita Gonzales, Mari Cruz, Jacinta Gonzales and Mari Loli (see page 111).

A photo of one of the ecstatic walks as spoken about in the book. Seen here is Conchita.

Photo of the "Little Miracle" of Garabandal, the miraculous Communion received by Conchita Gonzales. You can see the host on her tongue in this shot (see page 113)

Joey Lomangino, the man who is to have his eyes replaced
at the Miracle. You can see the damage that was done by
the tire explosion clearly in this picture, taken in 1975 (see
pages 115-116)

A picture of Blessed Padre Pio giving Joey his blessing.

DEPARTMENT OF THE ARMY
HEADQUARTERS UNITED STATES ARMY TRAINING AND DOCTRINE COMMAND
FORT MONROE, VIRGINIA 23651-5000

REPLY TO
ATTENTION OF

S: 29 August 1994

27 July 1994

ATBO-KM

MEMORANDUM FOR SEE DISTRIBUTION

SUBJECT: Draft Army Regulation on Civilian Inmate Labor Program

1. Enclosed for your review and comment is the draft Army
regulation on civilian inmate labor utilization and establishing
prison camps on Army installations. The draft regulation is the
compilation of all policy message, Civilian Inmate Labor
Oversight Committee policy decisions, and lessons learned to
date. The new regulation will provide the following:

   a. Policy for civilian inmate utilization on installations.

   b. Procedures for preparing requests to establish civilian
inmate labor programs on installations.

   c. Procedures for preparing requests to establish civilian
prison camps on installations.

2. The regulation will not be official until the printed copies
are distributed. Therefore, draft should not be circulated as an
official document.

3. Please forward your comments on DA Form 2028 (Recommended
Changes to Publications and Blank Forms) to HQ TRADOC, ATTN:
ATBO-KM/Gerri Rumbough, Fort Monroe, Virginia 23651-5000 NLT 29
August 1994. Further, request you provide the name of your point
of contact to Gerri Rumbough upon receipt of this memorandum (DSN
680-5189/COMM (804) 728-5189 or PROFS MON1(RUMBOUGG).

FOR THE COMMANDER:

1 Encl
as

                            charles D. Sprull
                         FOR C. DEAN RHODY
                             Director
                             Resource Management

Actual United States Army document that confirms the
existence of civilian prison camps (see page 143)

Photos taken at Fort Dix, New Jersey, of an alleged civilian internment camp (see Chapter 12, pages 143-155)

Another photo of the camp at Fort Dix.

Portable jail cells that can be transported on flatbed trucks.

FEMA has divided the country into ten regions. This map shows what those regions are (see pages 148-149)

The Jacinta 1972 picture taken in 1971 at Queens, New York: This picture supposedly contains the date, year and hour of the coming Chastisement (see pages 192-193)

End-Time Supply Information

You can contact Boler Technology for most of the herbs mentioned in this book. Please note that the author does not profit from the sales of these items and has no connection with this company.

Boler Technologies
4145 Shadow Lane #429
Santa Rosa,CA, 95405
Phone: 1-866-603-3265 ext. 3

USEFUL PRAYERS

Apostles Creed

I believe in God, the Father Almighty, creator of Heaven and Earth and in Jesus Christ, His only Son, Our Lord. Who was conceived by the Holy Ghost, born of the Virgin Mary, suffered under Pontius Pilot, was crucified, died and was buried. He descended into Hell and on the third day he rose again from the dead. He ascended into Heaven and is seated at the right hand of God, the Father Almighty, from thence he shall come to judge the living and the dead. I believe in the Holy Ghost, the Holy Catholic Church, the communion of Saints, the forgiveness of sins, the resurrection of the body and life everlasting. Amen.

The Our Father

Our Father, who art in heaven, hallowed be Thy Name. Thy kingdom come, thy will be done, on earth as it is in heaven. Give us this day our daily bread and forgive us our trespasses, as we forgive those who trespass against us and lead us not into temptation, but deliver us from evil. Amen.

Hail Mary

Hail Mary, full of grace, the Lord is with thee. Blessed art thou among women, and blessed is the fruit of thy womb, Jesus. Holy Mary, Mother of God, pray for us sinners, now and at the hour of our death. Amen.

Glory Be

Glory be to the Father and to the Son and to the Holy Ghost, as it was in the beginning, is now and ever shall be, world without end. Amen.

O My Jesus Prayer

O my Jesus, forgive us our sins and save us from the fires of hell. Lead all souls to heaven, especially those in most need of Thy mercy.

Hail Holy Queen

Hail, Holy Queen, mother of mercy, our life, our sweetness and our hope. To thee do we cry, poor banished children of Eve. To thee do we send up our sighs, mourning and weeping in this valley of tears. Turn then, most gracious advocate, thine eyes of mercy towards us and after this our exile, show unto us the blessed fruit of Thy Womb, Jesus. O clement, O loving, O sweet Virgin Mary. Pray for us O Holy Mother of God, that we may be made worthy of the promises of Christ. Amen.

St. Michael Prayer

St. Michael, the Archangel, defend us in battle. Be our defense against the wickedness and snares of the devil. May God rebuke him we humbly pray, and do thou, O Prince of the heavenly host, by the power of God, thrust into hell Satan and all the evil spirits who prowl about the world, seeking the ruin of souls. Amen.

Guardian Angel Prayer

Angel of God, my guardian dear, to whom God's love commits me here, ever this day (or night) be at my side, to light, to guard, to rule, to guide. Amen.

The Memorare

Remember, O most gracious Virgin Mary, that never was it known, that anyone who fled to thy protection, implored thy help or asked for thy aid was left unaided. Inspired by this confidence, I fly unto thee, O Virgin of Virgins, my Mother. To thee do I come, before thee I stand, sinful and sorrowful. O Mother of the Word Incarnate, despise not my petition, but in thy clemency, hear and answer me. Amen.

Act Of Contrition

O my God, I am heartily sorry for having offended thee. I detest all my sins because I dread the loss of heaven and the pains of hell, but most of all because they offend thee, my God, who art all good and deserving of all my love. I firmly resolve, with the help of Thy grace, to confess my sins, to do penance and to amend my life. Amen.

The Divine Mercy Chaplet
For use on a regular rosary

Make the sign of the cross. Say one Our Father, one Hail Mary and one Apostles Creed. On the large beads, say the following prayer:

Eternal Father, I offer you the body and blood, soul and divinity of Thy dearly beloved Son, Our Lord, Jesus Christ in atonement for our sins and those of the whole world.

On the small beads, say the following prayer:

For the sake of His sorrowful passion, have mercy on us and on the whole world.

On the remaining beads, say the following prayer three times:

Holy God, Holy mighty One, Holy Immortal One, have mercy on us and on the whole world.

Make the sign of the cross.

The Fifteen Promises Of Mary To Christians Who Recite The Rosary

Given To St. Dominic

- Whoever shall faithfully serve me by the recitation of the rosary shall receive signal graces.

- I promise my special protection and the greatest graces to all those who shall recite the rosary.

- The rosary shall be a powerful armor against hell, it will destroy vice, decrease sin, and defeat heresies.

- It will cause virtue and good works to flourish; it will obtain for souls the abundant mercy of God; It will withdraw the hearts of men from the love of the world and it's vanities, and it will lift them to the desire of eternal things. Oh, that the soul would sanctify themselves by this means.

- The soul which recommends itself to me by the recitation of the rosary, shall not perish.

- Whoever shall recite the rosary devoutly, applying himself to the consideration of its sacred mysteries shall never be conquered by misfortune. God will not chastise him in His justice, he shall not perish by an unprovided death; if he be just he shall remain in the grace of God, and become worthy of eternal life.

- Whoever shall have a true devotion for the rosary shall not die without the sacraments of the Church.

- Those who are faithful to recite the rosary shall have during their life and at their death the light of God and the plenitude of His graces; at the moment of death they shall participate in the merits of the saints in paradise.

- I shall deliver from purgatory those who have been devoted to the rosary.

- The faithful children of the rosary shall merit a higher degree of glory in Heaven.

- You shall obtain all you ask of me by the recitation of the rosary.

- All those who propagate the holy rosary shall be aided by me in their necessities.

- I have obtained from my Divine Son that all the advocates of the rosary shall have for intercessors the entire celestial court during life and at the hour of their death.

- All who recite the rosary are my sons, and brothers of my only son Jesus Christ.

- Devotion to my rosary is a great sign of predestination.

For more information on basic prayers, how to say the rosary and other devotions, please contact:

The Workers Of Our Lady Of Mount Carmel
Po Box 606
Lindenhurst, NY 11757
613-226-4408

Bibliography

AA – 1025 The Memoirs of an Anti-Apostle, by Marie Carre, Tan Books and Publishing, 1991

Against Heresies, by St. Iranaeus

Dimensions, by Jacques Vallee, Contemporary Books, 1988

Divine Institutes, by St. Lacantius

Divine Mercy in My Soul, by Sister Faustina, Marians of the Immaculate Conception, 1996

Douay Rheims Bible, Tan Books and Publishing, 1989

End Time Food List and Preparations, Freitag Publishing 1999

Everything You Always Wanted to Know About Prophecy, by Jack Van Impe, JVI Ministries

Federal Reserve Board Testimony of Allan Greenspan, 1998

Garabandal Magazine, Joey's Story, The Workers of Our Lady of Mount Carmel, 1998

King James Bible, Zondervan Publishing House, 1991

Le Secret De Melanie, by Abbe Combe, 1904

New Lies For Old, by Anatoly Golitsyn, G.S.G. & Associates, 1990

Our Lady of the Roses, Apostles of Our Lady, Inc. 1993

Perhaps Today Newsletter, 1996 Edition, Jack Van Impe Ministries

Roman Catechism

Roses From Heaven, Children of Mary, Inc. 1990

Summa Theologica, by St. Thomas Aquinas

The Apocalyptic Ark, The Order of St. Charbel

The Catholic Encyclopedia VIII, Robert Appleton Co. 1910

The Final Hour, by Michael Brown, Faith Publishing Company, 1992

The Last Pope, by John Hogue, Element Books, 1998

The Last Secret of Fatima Revealed, by Brother Michael of the Holy Trinity.

The Life of Anne Catherine Emmerich, by Carl Shmoger, Tan Books and Publishing, 1992

These Last Days Newsletter, TLDM Ministries

Through the Eyes of the Enemy, by Stanislav Lunev, Regnery Publishing, Inc. 1998

To The Priests, by Father Gobbi, Marian Movement of Priests, 1996

White House Press Library

Workers of Our Lady of Mount Carmel

Photo Credits

The author and publisher wish to thank the following people for providing us with the permission to use their photographs for which they hold the copyright.

Andrew Wingate – Invasion Map.

Gary Wohlsheid, These Last Days Ministries - Papal pictures, voice recordings and Jacinta 1972 picture.

Newswatch Magazine – Internment camp photographs.

The Workers of Our Lady of Mount Carmel – Photographs of Joey Lomangino, Padre Pio and the Garabandal Seers.

INDEX

D

H

T

About The Author

Kathleen Keating is an investigative journalist. She runs the premier Internet news site, Strategic Jungle Syndicate, and publishes a monthly newsletter, The Messenger, bringing the world the latest end-time breaking reports.

Kathleen writes an immensely popular weekly Internet column, The Keating Perspective, and spends what remaining time she has left every day working on her exhaustive research and her upcoming books.

Visit Kathleen's websites at:

Strategic Jungle Syndicate
www.strategicjungle.com

The Messenger
www.materdeipress.com

Kathleen's website
www.kathleenkeating.com

Did You Enjoy This Book?
Than you may enjoy the following titles
By Kathleen Keating

- ➢ The Gates of Hell: All Roads Lead To Rome

- ➢ Torn Sky, a novel based on the research behind The Final Warning

- ➢ Noise of The Mourning, the book that started it all

- ➢ Silence of the Evening, the spectacular sequel to Noise of The Mourning

Call 1-866-394-BOOK (2665)
to order these books or Kathleen's monthly newsletter,
The Messenger. Get up to the minute information on what's
going on behind the scenes with prophecy, politics and
people!